Dr. Michael A. Freeman

MARRIAGE MADE EZ IN 31 DAYS

Copyright ©2012 FIG Publishing
www.FIGPublishing.com

All Rights Reserved. No part of this book may be reproduced, stored in a retrieval system or transmitted in any form or by any means, electronic, mechanical, photocopying, recording or otherwise, except for the inclusion of brief quotations in a review, without prior permission in writing from the publisher.

Unless otherwise noted, scripture quotations are taken from the *Holy Bible,* King James Version.

Book design by: GreeneHouse Media, Print Division

ISBN: 978- 0-9828180-2-2

FIG Publishing
12138 Central Avenue, #464
Mitchellville, Maryland 20721
1.888.202.6766
www.FIGPublishing.com
info@FIGPublishing.com

ACKNOWLEDGEMENTS

In preparation of this work, which will bless many people and marriages throughout the world, DeeDee and I are very grateful for the inspiration, wisdom and example of many great men and women, including, but not limited to, the following:

Bishop Robert O. and Mother Carrie B. Freeman and Mr. and Mrs. James and Celestine Wooten, our parents, for their 62-year commitment to marriage. You have served as conduits of commitment for us.

Apostle Frederick K.C. Price and Dr. Betty Price, for their continual, exemplary standards concerning the sanctity of the marriage covenant. We love, honor and greatly appreciate you both.

Mr. and Mrs. Richard Smith, for their leadership and loyalty to us, to ministry and upholding a standard of righteousness before all of the couples of Spirit of Faith Christian Center and their assisting in perpetuating the standards of marriage.

The partners of Spirit of Faith Christian Center for their support and love throughout the years.

Ms. Katrina Ferguson. Thank you for making this entire project effortless for us.

All of those with whom we met to get their counsel and input on this project. Thank you for your time and Godly counsel.

All of the married couples that have joined this crusade.

TABLE OF CONTENTS

INTRODUCTION

For many years I have both believed and taught that the heart is the birthplace for all of the increase in our lives; for out of the heart flow the forces of life. This book is my opportunity to speak to your hearts concerning the relationship and covenant of marriage, as well as to discuss some of the challenges and questions that we face in our marriages that cause the relationship to be difficult, rather than easy.

My purpose in writing this book is to forge an assault on the alarmingly high divorce rate by creating a manual that will assist couples in partaking of their God-given right to a loving marriage and God's intent for them to enjoy each other through and in their marriages. It's obvious that two people coming from different backgrounds will have disagreements and misunderstandings, but that doesn't have to result in non-stop chaos, conflict, and dissolution of the marriage. God wants your marriage to work and so do I.

It's an easily understood philosophy that if you want what someone else has or desire to do what someone else has done, then you need to find out their strategy and their plan for doing it and copy them. It is okay to be a copy-cat as long as you are copying the right cat! For instance, if you were endeavoring to become one of the richest people in our nation, it just makes sense that you would seek opportunities to speak to the wealthiest people in the country, such as Bill Gates, Carlos Slim or Warren Buffett. If endeavoring to excel in the game of golf, undoubtedly, you would emulate the practice routines of Tiger Woods, Phil Mickelson, or even Arnold Palmer. If endeavoring to become one of America's top television talk show hosts, you would want to glean from Oprah Winfrey or Larry King. With that in mind, as you are endeavoring to enhance and improve your marriage, you should definitely seek the wisdom and counsel of individuals who have successful and thriving marriages.

Although I don't believe I have *all* of the answers, I do have a successful and thriving marriage. In more than 26 years of being married to DeeDee, we have experienced both the very good and the very bad. As a result, there are insights that I have been assigned to share with the Body of Christ concerning this covenant called marriage. My motto for years has been, "Get around those who have your answer and get away from those that have your problem." When it comes to marriage, surely this book will provide you with answers to whatever challenges are stopping you from a ***Marriage Made EZ***.

DeeDee and I have declared war on divorce and we want you to join us in this revolution. For the next 31 days you will be in our boot camp, office, home, and car getting the information and the inspiration we have gained through years of marriage experience. It's like meeting with us for the next 31 days. In doing so, I am positive we can help you make your marriage easier.

Just to be clear, marriage is **WORK**! Decide today to do the work for a great marriage knowing that anything worth having is worth working for. My use of the word "*work*" here should not deter you, but rather prepare you for what is ahead. I'll be giving you step-by-step instructions. If you adhere to the instructions, you will experience marriage as God intended it from the very beginning, hence, your *Marriage Made EZ*.

Allow me to give you a bit of our history. When we first met, DeeDee was 14 and I was 16. Having heard a lot about each other, a mutual interest was sparked and we wanted to meet. That opportunity finally came when I visited the local swimming pool where she was working. There are very few things I remember about our first encounter. However, I do remember telling her, "Hey girl, leave that squirrel and come see the world with me;" and then I asked, "What's your sign?" I had game back then. Believe it or not, at that time, she was interested in another guy, even at her young age. (I guess we will call it puppy love.) We were in and out of each other's lives until our early 20's, when we finally married in 1985. Here we are, more than 26 years later, experiencing God's best as our marriage has been made EZ. Lord knows, it hasn't always been that way.
Both DeeDee's parents and my parents have been married for more than 61 years. That amounts to more than 122 years of marital commitment. It is obvious that in those 122 years there have been differences, disappointments, misunderstandings, problems, and outright "intense fellowship" (i.e., brawls). However, a force bigger and more powerful than our parents caused them to stay together.

We have also had the privilege of gleaning from the relationships of prominent couples in the body of Christ, namely the late Bishop James & Apostle Betty Peebles married over 40 years, Drs. Fred & Betty Price married over 56 years, and others who have meant a great deal to us. So, in addition to our parents, you can clearly see that we have had access to several couples who have experienced a great deal of success in marriage; all of whom have been married to the same spouse and have never experienced divorce. (This in itself is a principle that we will discuss later in this book as we talk about associations). So it is clear that you can have what the Scriptures say you can have -

one man and one woman joined in holy matrimony until they are parted by death.

Although I have commonly stated this in times past, even in this chapter, it bears repeating: marriage is something you don't get out of alive. You are bound to your spouse for the rest of your life. For that reason, let's work together to create a *Marriage Made EZ*, worthy of imitation in your lives. God desires that your marriage be held up in His hand as a trophy to show the world what He intended for marriage to look like from the very beginning.

Let's get started!

HOW TO USE THIS BOOK

Many couples come to us and say things like, "God didn't see fit to fix my marriage." He wasn't supposed to. He has given us everything we need to fix our own marriages. Let's take matters in our own hands and deal with our issues. DeeDee and I are no different than you. We were programmed, and thereby destined, to fail in marriage. Everything around us programs us to fail. In the 80s, most television shows depicted strong families and marriages. Today's shows depict the opposite. (Make no mistake: it is called television *programming* for the purpose of controlling the thinking of the viewer.) This book is about reprogramming our thinking and our actions so that we can live *Marriage Made EZ.*

It's time to (re)engage your spouse on a path to *Marriage Made EZ.* Along with your Bible, this book is your personal reference manual to create success in your marriage. It can be used for your personal marriage or even as discussion material for your small groups or couples' ministry. All scriptures are quoted from the King James Version, unless otherwise noted.

Marriage Made EZ is formatted as a step-by-step guide for you and your spouse to follow at least for the next 31 days. I recommend *strongly* that you go through this material over and over again until it becomes a part of you, second nature if you will. My guarantee is that if you will walk with me through these principles for *Marriage Made EZ,* in the order I laid out, you will see tremendous growth in your marriage. For the sake of clarity, here are your steps:

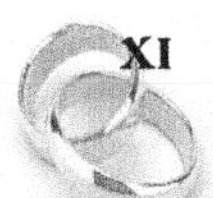

1. Read each day consecutively, in order, as laid out in this book. Do not skip around or look for a topic that grabs your attention.

2. Meditate on the scriptures day and night "... that thou mayest observe to do according to all that is written therein: for then thou shalt make thy way prosperous, and then thou shalt have good success." (Joshua 1:8, KJV).

3. Confession creates and brings possession. Make the confessions for each day throughout the day "... with the mouth confession is made unto salvation." (Romans 10:10, KJV).

4. Do the exercises, sometimes with, and other times without, your spouse "... faith without works is dead." (James 2:20, KJV).

5. And finally, record your thoughts on the pages provided at the end of the text for each day "... write the vision and make it plain upon tables, that he may run that readeth it." (Habakkuk 2:2, KJV).

Your goal of *Marriage Made EZ* will be more easily accomplished through having the opportunity to learn from the experiences of someone who has already achieved what you are attempting to accomplish. Thank God, you no longer have to walk this journey alone. I will be your coach, your mentor, your drill sergeant, and your cheerleader while my marriage to DeeDee serves as your model and inspiration. It is my prayer and my belief that through your diligence, discipline, determination, and

commitment to mastering this material, you will experience God's perfect plan for your marriage - a *Marriage Made EZ.*

Once again, commit to read this book, in its entirety, in order. It has been written methodically, as a step-by-step process. Resist the urge to start in the middle or with a topic that grabs your attention. Start at the beginning and go day-to-day. If you will commit to doing so, sign here, have your spouse do the same and let's get started in making your *Marriage EZ*.

On this, the 28th day of July, 2015, we commit to follow the above instructions and read this book in its entirety, as it is written. We have opened our hearts and minds to hear from God along this journey and choose to do the work necessary to achieve our goal of a marriage worthy of imitation, a trophy to show the world what He intended marriage to look like from the very beginning.

____________________ ____________________

Husband *Wife*

DAY 1:

THE CORE OF MARRIAGE - JESUS IS THE ANSWER TO MARRIAGE MADE EZ - *NOT*

For so long, we have been taught, even from some of the most prestigious pulpits in the world, that Jesus is the answer to everything that ails us. Whether it is our relationship, our children and, consequently, our lives, we have turned and pointed a finger at Jesus, making Him responsible for what we are responsible. This is where we dismantle that belief system; where we dispel the misnomer, the mindset that Jesus is the answer, the reason for the current condition of our marriage. God sacrificed His own son, and Jesus sacrificed His very life so that we can live victoriously here on earth. What more is there for Him to do? He's done everything for us and given us everything that we need. Now, it's totally up to us to subdue the earth... to take control of our circumstances.

Genesis 1:28(MSG) – "And God blessed them, and God said unto them, Be fruitful, and multiply, and replenish the earth, and subdue it: and have dominion over the fish of the sea, and over the fowl of the air, and over every living thing that moveth upon the earth."

Unfortunately, many of us have used these teachings as ways to avoid taking personal responsibility for what goes on in our relationships as excuses to not do our part. Later in this book, we will talk about our specific roles in marriage. For now, it is important to declare our marriages as excuse-free zones. Meaning, we don't make excuses for our shortcomings, and instead, we purpose to get better, to grow stronger and to be more effective in our marriages. It's time out for making excuses in order to somehow support our shortcomings.

With our personal responsibility in mind, we now know that Jesus is not the answer, yet He is at the center, the core of our marriages. Let's look more closely at how Webster's defines core:

Core: **a :** a basic, essential, or enduring part (as of an individual, a class, or an entity) <the staff had a *core* of experts> <the *core* of her beliefs>**b :** the essential meaning **:** GIST <the *core* of the argument>**c :** the inmost or most intimate part <honest to the *core*>

Core**:** a central and often foundational part usually distinct from the enveloping part by a difference in nature <the *core* of the city>

Interesting. So the core is the central, innermost and most essential part of anything. Think apple core. Think of our heart being the very core of our being and marriage being the core foundation of families, communities, and societies around the globe.

The Word of God says to guard our hearts because out of them flow the very issues of our lives. This is an indication that the core of anything is as crucial to its existence and its well-being, as Jesus is to our marriage. And, if marriage in the earth realm represents Christ in the heavenlies and His relationship to the

Body of Christ, then we must reconsider our priorities and how we relate to each other in marriage.

For many, now that we understand who Christ is in our marriage, we must discover how to take advantage of His positioning. In other words, how do we benefit from Christ being at the core of our marriages? We must recognize and acknowledge the true identity of the individuals in the marriage, including their belief systems, their personal relationships with Jesus, their relationship with each other, and who or what is currently at the core of this marriage. In other words, the only hope to ever achieve your goal is that you and your spouse recognize and acknowledge that Jesus is NOT the reason that your marriage isn't flourishing, nor is He the reason that your marriage is in trouble. It's you, both of you. We must take personal responsibility for the state of our marriage. Until we do so, there is little, if any, hope for a *Marriage Made EZ.*

Let's analyze to what it is I am referring. First and foremost, each spouse must have his or her own separate and distinct relationship with Jesus. Each spouse must do the following:

(1) accept Jesus as his/her Lord and Savior as Romans 10:9-10 says, "[9]That if thou shalt confess with thy mouth the Lord Jesus, and shalt believe in thine heart that God hath raised him from the dead, thou shalt be saved. [10]For with the heart man believeth unto righteousness; and with the mouth confession is made unto salvation."

(2) accept His gift of the Holy Spirit and its power as evidenced first by the speaking of tongues as Acts 1:8 reads, "[8]But ye shall receive power, after that the Holy Ghost is come upon you: and ye shall be witnesses unto me both in Jerusalem, and in all Judaea, and in Samaria, and unto the uttermost part of the earth."

(3) acknowledge that the Bible is the inspired Word of God and have accepted it as the instruction manual for life as stated in 2 Timothy 3:16, "All scripture is given by inspiration of God, and is profitable for doctrine, for reproof, for correction, for instruction in righteousness."

With that understanding and agreement, it becomes easier to relate to and understand our spouse because we have the third person of the Holy Trinity involved. Often there are times where you don't really fully understand or agree with their message, but because you have Jesus at the center of the relationship and you're both committed to Him and His will for your marriage, you can find the strength to remain together. So now, when things are not warm and fuzzy, and you and your spouse are not tiptoeing through the tulips, you have the ability to go back and figure out what happened. Because we have the insight of Holy Spirit, we can minister more effectively to the needs of our spouse. We can now address all the issues that concern us because we have made God's priorities our own.

Psalm 127:1 reads, "Except the Lord build the house, they labor in vain that build it..." For years I never really understood this Scripture; however, I received illumination while building our home. The meaning of this Scripture was never more evident to me than at that time. The contractor gave me the blueprints and said, "This is your house." He showed me where every room would be and how it all would be laid out. At that moment it hit me. This is just what our Heavenly Father has done. He has laid out blueprints in the Word for a blessed life, a blessed family, and a blessed marriage. If we adhere to His blueprints and build our house accordingly, our labor will never be in vain. However, when we divert from the blueprint, the Scripture clearly says that we labor in vain. You cannot accept random counsel from the barber shop, hair salon, gymnasium, locker room, or even some close relatives and expect to build the house God designed for you to live in.

Scripture (KJV)

Colossians 1:16 "For by him were all things created, that are in heaven, and that are in earth, visible and invisible, whether they be thrones or dominions, or principalities, or powers: all things were created by him, and for him:"

Exercise

Renew your commitment to Jesus today. Then renew your commitment to your spouse. Using your own words, confess to your spouse your belief that your marriage will grow and flourish as a result of the work that you are prepared to do. Pray together and call forth the oneness in your marriage that God intended. Hug and kiss and prepare yourselves for a life-altering experience. Be sure to record your commitment on the following pages.

Confession

I take responsibility for the state of my marriage, and I am responsible for my own happiness and state of mind. I honor God and my spouse by committing to do the work in this book to have a *Marriage Made EZ.*

____

____

____

____

____

Do not make excuses for our shortcomings
Purpose to get better, grow stronger
pray together

DAY 2:

THE PURPOSE OF MARRIAGE - LEAVE, CLEAVE, AND WEAVE

The enjoyment of anything and its intended goal will be discovered in its purpose. From the beginning of time, the intent of marriage was for it to be enjoyed by two people: a man and a woman. Let me repeat myself... one man and one woman. That was, is, and will forever be God's plan for marriage. God intended for marriage to represent God on earth – to reveal God to the world as one. According to Genesis, man and woman together form the image of God. The dominion mandate makes it clear that man and woman must come together and work together to take dominion of the world. He intended for marriage to be His answer to the perpetuation of His extended family in the earth. Undoubtedly, it is the desire of satan, the enemy of our soul, to warp and permanently destroy God's original plan for humanity through the violation of this sacred covenant. He uses our natural frailties, weaknesses, lusts, and fleshly desires against us to pursue sinful activities that ultimately undermine God's Will for our marriages and our lives.

So, when was the last time you asked God about the purpose for your marriage? I'm not talking about the "go forth and multiply" generic purpose. I'm talking about the purpose for which God ordained *that* man or *that* woman for your life. What skills, gifts,

or talents do you possess as a couple that will bless the Body of Christ? What are you destined to create together that you could never accomplish alone?

The reason God created marriage between one man and one woman is so their collective abilities would complement each other in marriage and in life. That's why same-sex marriages don't work. First, they are not ordained or sanctioned by God; second, they are not blessed by God; third, they do not fulfill the requirements of contributions, unity, and balance that come from the joining of male and female together. Homosexuality is sin because it is out of balance and out of sync with God's Word, His purpose, and intent for marriage. In the beginning God created man and woman, he and she, not he and him. During one of our services, I shared an illustration with our partners. Using a heavy duty extension cord that had both male ends, I showed how without the female connector, there is no way for the power to flow through the cord from the intended source to the place where the power is needed. It's the same way for same-sex relationships. They are improper and stunt the flow of power from God to and through the relationship.

Leave, Cleave, and Weave is the subtitle of many sermons and wedding messages all across the country. This message underscores the plan God established for marriage and outlines the priorities that are to take place in the relationship. In scripture, a man is instructed to leave the home and care of his mother and father; to cleave unto his wife; and to weave their lives together as one. The fact that many spouses have not completely undertaken the process to "leave, cleave, and weave" is undoubtedly the source of countless arguments, fights, and marital discord. Let's look at each of these individually.

The idea of leaving your parents is not about abandoning, ignoring, or neglecting them. It's about priorities. The Bible instructs husbands to "leave" in the sense of proximity and order, not love or concern. Having a close relationship with our parents is a wonderful thing. And having a close relationship with our in-laws is the ideal situation – one many people never even dream possible. However, "leaving" your parents means that your first priority and obligation is to your husband or wife. Mom's input on how your marriage should work should not and cannot override the input of your wife. Conversely, dad's input on how a household should run should not and cannot overshadow the way your husband manages and runs his own household. Attempting to reconcile differing opinions between parents and spouses is dangerous and destructive to marriages.

Cleaving means to "stick together like glue" -- to not be easily separated, like grains of sand. Genesis 2:24 says, "Therefore shall a man leave his father and his mother, and shall cleave unto his wife: and they shall be one flesh." This speaks to the oneness that must be accomplished in marriage.

Once you follow Godly instructions to leave and cleave, the next step is to weave your lives together. To weave means to interlace as if you were forming a fabric. You are creating the very fabric of your lives that includes spiritual agreement, prayer, worship, vision, goals, and family endeavors. It is through these steps that couples should weave their lives together as one. Becoming one does not mean losing your identity or independence as an individual; it means that you unite your vision and purpose toward a common goal with your spouse and focus solely on accomplishing the God-given purpose for your marriage.

Scripture (KJV)

Jeremiah 29:11 "For I know the thoughts that I think toward you, saith the Lord, thoughts of peace, and not of evil, to give you an expected end."

Mark 10:7-9 "For this cause shall a man leave his father and mother, and cleave to his wife; And they twain shall be one flesh: so then they are no more twain, but one flesh. What therefore God hath joined together, let not man put asunder."

Exercise

Do something for your spouse today that will create closeness in your marriage. Whether it's leaving a note on your spouse's pillow when you leave for work or sending them flowers during the day. Do something that will touch his/her heart and let him/her know that you're committed to your promise to love, honor, and cherish him/her. Record what you did and your spouse's reaction on the following pages.

Confession

Knowing that God has a purpose for my marriage, I cleave to my spouse and we are one flesh. We always agree. No issue, topic, or challenge interferes with our unity.

We always agree - not realistic!

Both educated in different areas, can help each other work things out based on expertise.

Both strong and bull headed at times which causes friction.

Jay is better at handling anger but suppressing it can cause friction.

Tasha is not as good with handling anger or being overly opinionated and can think things over more clearly before reacting.

DAY 3: COVENANT - A PROMISE IS A PROMISE

For many people, the change in times has brought with it a change in the way they look at the covenant relationship of marriage. The Bible clearly states that the word "marriage" identifies a lifelong commitment between a man and a woman. This view does not leave space for divorce or other situations, such as extramarital affairs or shacking (i.e., living with someone that you are not married to). Unfortunately, in today's society, the rate of divorce has reached an all-time high. Surprisingly, this statistic is not only alarming in the world system, but also in the church, in spite of the fact that God hates divorce. There are many challenges contributing to the rate of divorce in our land, few of which actually present a biblical basis for divorce. In the book of Mark 10:5, Jesus said that the only reason there has even been a provision made for divorce is due to "the hardness of men's hearts."

Husbands and wives, this is big boy and big girl stuff. It is time to grow up and be "determined soldiers" in the fight for our marriages. As Christians, we need to declare war on divorce and go back to the beginning with "Relationship Basic Training." In the military, all new recruits are required to attend boot camp to help them to achieve a higher level of discipline and to toughen

them up. During that experience, they must swear by oath to uphold the Constitution of the United States of America. Based on the recent divorce rates, husbands and wives need to do the same thing. Marriage is not for the faint of heart and just like in the military, you must be disciplined and committed to seeing the mission through to the end based on your sworn oath to love, honor, and cherish your spouse until death do you part. Remember, it's not about the feeling, it's about the commitment. Your word must be your bond because without it, you have nothing.

Marriage is a full and total commitment to serve and love another person. It's not just a ceremony with some vows; it is a "covenant" between a man, a woman and God. When things don't go our way in marriage, we can't just take our toys and run away, or take our ball and go home. Ecclesiastes 5:5 tells us that it's "Better to not make a vow at all, than to make a vow and not honor it." The time is up for playing relationship games. We have to stand up and take authority over whatever threatens to derail or destroy the commitments that we made. Marriage is a relationship for life… so let's start living and enjoy being married.

Additionally, it is God's intent that no one get out of marriage alive. Say it with me, "Marriage is something I do not get out of of alive." "Until death do us part" is not just a quaint statement. It is a commandment by God Almighty to those of us who have said, "I do" in response to a covenant of which we've agreed to be a part.

> **Covenant** - noun**:** a usually formal, solemn, and binding agreement **:**
>
> a written agreement or promise usually under seal between two or more parties especially for the

performance of some action : the common-law action to recover damages for breach of such a contract

verb : to promise by a covenant : PLEDGE

The Bible is filled with examples of covenants between God and individuals like Adam, Abraham, Noah, and David. The covenant was an agreement and a pledge that God presented to establish His kingdom and bless His people. Covenants are bigger than the people involved, greater than the sum of their parts. They are used to encourage a nation or bless a generation, and your marriage is no different.

Marriage is a covenant designed to create "oneness." That means that no matter what the topic, issue, or difficulty, the two spouses should be able to come together as ONE. That doesn't mean that you're the exact same person or that you don't have differences in your thought process and approach. What it means is that you both have a Christ-centered life that relies on His Word to direct you. Since there is one perfect Will of God for your marriage, both of you ultimately should come to the same conclusion through the leading and direction of the Holy Spirit. The key comes in the form of an "agreement." The power of agreement in marriage is phenomenal. "The Father, Son, and Holy Spirit are in such perfect agreement because they are ONE." That should be the goal for your marriage.

During their marriage ceremonies, many couples use a separated 3-strand cord to symbolize the coming together of their lives. Together, at the altar, they braid the cords together to show their unity, the weaving of their individual lives around Jesus as the center. This tradition serves as a visual reminder of their oneness.

Scriptures (KJV):

1 John 4:4 "... because greater is he that is in you, than he that is in the world."

1 John 5:4 "For whatsoever is born of God overcometh the world: and this is the victory that overcometh the world, even our faith."

Romans 8:37 "Nay, in all these things we are more than conquerors through him that loved us."

Ecclesiastes 5:5 "Better is it that thou shouldest not vow, than that thou shouldest vow and not pay."

Exercise

Use the rope or cord that you purchased to have your own 'renewal of vows' ceremony as the two of you braid 3-strands together. Hang it prominently in your home as a reminder of the commitment you are making to keep your marriage together forever.

Confession

Renew your vows with your spouse today. If you don't have the actual vows that you said at your wedding, either write your own or use the following.

Husbands:

I have taken you to be my wife; I love you with all my heart. Out of all of the ladies on this planet God brought you into my life, and I have found you to be special, and I enjoy the covenant of marriage we have made. God has given us a wonderful family, His favor, and a future of purpose. I reaffirm my commitment to love you, to protect you, to provide for you, and to be exclusively yours all the days of my life. I covenant to lead our family in the ways of righteousness and by faith walk in God's best in every situation. I will continue to live before you and my children as a man of God that you can respect, trust, and follow. And together we will glorify God with our lives!

Wives:

I love you with all my heart and I thank God for bringing you into my life. I have accepted you as my husband. Out of all the men on this planet, I have found you to be special and I, too, enjoy the covenant of marriage we have entered into. Today, I reaffirm my commitment to love you and to be your wife. I believe you love me, I believe you will protect me, and I believe you will continue to provide for me and our children and you can count on me being exclusively yours all the days of my life. You can count on me to stand with you in every situation and, by faith, we will always have God's best! I too will continue to live as a woman of God that you and our children can respect and together we will glorify God with our lives!

____

____

____

____

____

____

____

____

DAY 4:
MY RESPONSE IS MY RESPONSIBILITY

In marriage, your response is your responsibility, and your responsibility is to respond properly based on God's Word and your spouse's needs. How you choose to respond to a situation, difficulty, or conflict is just that: your choice. Life is governed by choices and you (and your marriage) will live or die based on the choices that you make. For Christians, more specifically, life is a series of Spirit-led decisions; or at least, it should be. Even if you think you're not the reason for your relationship issues, you are an intricate part of its restoration and, as such, you still have to accept responsibility for helping repair what's broken and respond with the intention of healing, not hurting.

When we respond, we reply and affirm whatever was communicated to us. When we demonstrate ability, we prove our power or capability to handle a given situation. When we combine the two, we demonstrate our ability to properly respond and affirm the reality of any situation we may encounter in our marriage.

Throughout my entire service in ministry, I have never seen so many "isms" and "schisms" and a vast refusal of people to take personal responsibility for the consequences of their actions. These days it seems that everything wrong is somebody else's fault. People blame society, their upbringing, and various other societal ills instead of being accountable for their own lives. This is true in and out of the church. While many people blame "the system" or "the man" for their troubles, the Church is famous for blaming "the devil" or sitting back and "waiting on God" as an excuse for their inaction, failings, and shortcomings. There must come a time when you stop blaming others for your situation.

Marriage is no exception to this trend. Husbands who cheat blame the other woman for seducing them; they blame their wives for not meeting their needs; or they blame their circumstances for creating an environment that compelled them to lie, cheat, and dishonor their marriage vows. Wives who stray or leave their marriages blame their husbands for not meeting their expectations; they blame other women for tempting their husbands; and they blame being overwhelmed by life's responsibilities for pushing them out of the marriage. Nonsense.

Each one of us is where we are today as a result of the series of choices we made yesterday. Every decision we've faced came with a set of consequences of which we were aware. Even when life throws a curve ball, there is always a choice to make and those choices always have consequences. Sometimes the choices are good or bad; sometimes they are bad and bad; and in a few instances, they are bad or worse. However, the choice is still yours – as are the consequences and the need to accept those consequences.

Husbands, we are called to be the spiritual leaders in our homes. That means, ultimately, the accountability and responsibility for the success or failure in our home rests on our shoulders. We can continue to blame our wives, jobs, families, finances, etc., or we can accept ownership of our responsibility to lead our homes the way God instructed us to do. It's time to "man up."

Why is it so difficult to admit when we're wrong? This is especially true for men. How many men do you know who will admit when they're lost? Wouldn't it be easier to stop and ask for directions? Somehow, our sense of pride will not allow us to admit our error. And instead of taking responsibility for being lost, we'll waste precious time trying to prove that we're not lost. That same scenario plays out in life – for men and women. Instead of just admitting our mistakes and owning up to them, we'll drive around in emotional circles, blaming anything and everyone else, instead of just confessing the error of our ways.

Husbands and wives owe it to each other to be honest about accepting personal responsibility. If your marriage isn't what you want it to be, it's time to accept that some of that might be your fault. Yes, it takes two to tango and it takes two to argue. Typically, I say, "It takes two fools to fight. You don't have a fight with one fool. Which one will you be?" Confess. Repent. Forgive.

We must always be in a place where we respond rather than react. Reacting happens when we don't take the time or use the energy to think about what is really going on. Instead we relinquish control and react, often emotionally. Reacting creates stress, fear and anxiety and comes from a place of reflex rather than deliberation. Think first, act later.

Responding, on the contrary, defuses stress because we take the time to reason, to measure our solutions, and to make solid, lasting and effective choices. The key to staying in the mindset of responding rather than reacting is being prepared and disciplined enough to take a step back, in the moment, rather than reacting emotionally.

Knowing the differences, how do we grow to a place where we respond to our spouses rather than react to them? How do we assist our spouse in responding rather than reacting to us?

Simply put, knowing that as it is in the natural, it is in the spiritual; we must ensure that their emotional bank account is constantly in the black. When you go to the bank, you cannot make withdrawals until you have made deposits. Your account is in the black (positive) when you've put in more than you've taken out. Your account is in the red (negative) when you're overdrawn – or you've taken out more than you put in.

Relationships are much the same way. When you find your spouse reacting negatively, most often, it is an indication that they are suffering from being emotionally overdrawn and the bank fees you're being charged, in this instance, are unkind words and gestures. You must ensure that you make daily deposits into your spouse's emotional bank account with gestures of love and kindness. On the same token, you must also ensure that you maintain an adequate balance in your personal bank account by continually seeking God and His direction in every situation.

There was a day that I was so angry at DeeDee that as I was on my way home from work, I had decided that I was going to let her have it, "with both barrels", so to speak. I was prepared and armed for the argument of our relationship. When I walked in, I heard DeeDee praying in the spirit. I was totally deflated. How do you argue with someone who is seeking God? Needless to say, that was an argument that never happened. Where I was lacking in filling up her emotional bank account, God Himself had become her overdraft protection to keep her at peace. What a great God we serve!

It is easier to respond when you feel good about the relationship and your ability to work through problems and resolve them together. If your spouse is already on the defensive and doesn't have confidence in your ability to face challenges together, most likely he/she is going to react negatively to any distressing news or situation because the emotional place he/she is drawing from is filled with anxiety and frustration – two emotions that fuel negative reactions. Tomorrow we will begin to talk about effective communication wherein you will learn to take time to listen, hear, and comprehend what's being said. This will help strengthen your ability to respond to your spouse rather than reacting.

Scriptures (MSG)

Proverbs 15:18	"Hot tempers start fights; a calm, cool spirit keeps the peace."
Proverbs 16:32	"Moderation is better than muscle, self-control better than political power."

Scriptures (KJV)

James 1:19	"Wherefore, my beloved brethren, let every man be swift to hear, slow to speak, slow to wrath:"
James 1:22	"But be ye doers of the word, and not hearers only, deceiving your own selves."
Deuteronomy 30:19	"I call heaven and earth to record this day against you, that I have set before you life and death, blessing and cursing: therefore choose life, that both thou and thy seed may live:"
Hebrews 2:1	"Therefore we ought to give the more earnest heed to the things which we have heard, lest at any time we should let them slip."

Proverbs 15:33 "The fear of the Lord is the instruction of wisdom; and before honour is humility."

Proverbs 28:13 "He that covereth his sins shall not prosper: but whoso confesseth and forsaketh them shall have mercy."

Exercise

Sit down with your spouse and ask them to share their heart with you. Listen to him/her, without interrupting. Respond, rather than react. Responses begin with words like: "I hear what you're saying," or "Help me understand what you're feeling." Avoid reactions and judgments that sound similar to: "Why did you do that?" or "What were you thinking?" When the first person has finished speaking, then switch roles.

Think of a recent situation where you blamed someone else for your mistake. Confess it to God and to your spouse. Accept responsibility, ask for forgiveness, and then work to restore the situation.

Confession

I confess that I am not perfect, and I have made mistakes. I will take responsibility for my actions and be accountable to my spouse.

I listen to my spouse with a calm, cool spirit that keeps the peace, and I hear the entire matter before I speak so that I may respond appropriately.

How do we work through problems and resolve them together without arguing?

DAY 5:

THE COMMUNICATION PROCESS - CONNECTING THE DISCONNECTS IN MARRIAGE

Communication is the lifeblood of success in your marriage. It is so important that we will spend the next 3 days dealing with this topic, since your ability to communicate effectively will determine whether you will build up or tear down your marriage. We've all heard it said that perception is reality. When it comes to communicating effectively, often it's not about what you said, it's about what the other person heard, how they heard it, and how they interpreted what they heard. Communication is a process of creating meaning through interaction and is not successfully completed until all involved walk away with the same understanding. In order to ensure clear communication, you—as the communicator—need to confirm that your message has been received and understood.

The lack of proper communication is one of the most devastating, debilitating, and destructive components to the marriage relationship. It's actually the biggest challenge in most of the relationships that I have observed. Two people with two entirely different ways of communicating, placed under one roof, can be challenging in and of itself. That's why books like this one and others have been so popular. They illustrate the

communication gap between men and women and the difficulty in uniting people together in the absence of proper communication. Matthew 18:9 tells us that we must bridge the communication gap: "Again I say unto you, That if two of you shall agree on earth as touching anything that they shall ask, it shall be done for them of my Father which is in heaven."

Without communication, oneness is nearly impossible to achieve. Consider the biblical account of the events at the Tower of Babel. (Genesis 11) The inhabitants were productive, speaking a single language, when they came to Shinar and resolved to build a city with a tower "with its top in the heavens... lest we be scattered abroad upon the face of the Earth." When God saw what they were doing, He said, "They are one people and have one language, and nothing will be withholden from them which they purpose to do." So God confused their languages and scattered them over the earth, so that they could not fulfill their goal. Notice they were able to build whatever they could imagine when they were saying the same thing and had the same language. But when their languages clashed, work and progress ceased. There has been little progress in most relationships because couples don't understand each other, even when they are speaking the same language. Both people are speaking English, but they have two entirely different meanings for the same words. The ability to properly communicate will be one of the master keys that affect your relationship (and your life) either positively or negatively. My goal is to get you to say what you mean and mean what you say. The power to define is the power to fulfill. So many things are said one way, but interpreted with different meanings, thereby causing a different outcome than the one desired.

For instance, I asked DeeDee if she was going to get her hair done. Simple question, or so I thought. She got upset thinking I was saying that her hair didn't look good. In actuality, I was simply inquiring about her having a hair appointment. She interpreted something entirely different from what I meant, based upon how she had been conditioned to hear. Communication is only fulfilled when both the speaker and the listener understand the same thing. Remember, we are products of our environment, teachers, associates, and backgrounds and they have shaped how we hear.

What I learned in the process of growing our relationship is that communication is not so much about talking; it's more about exploration and preparation. During the communication process, we must explore our spouse's thoughts and ideas by listening, sharing, and asking questions. Communication is not just about how you talk; it's more about how the recipient of your communications listens. Sometimes effective communication is based on preparation. For instance, I am very analytical and DeeDee is not. In the exploration process, DeeDee realized that for me to be receptive to what she was communicating, she had to say things a certain way and at a certain time. At the beginning of a conversation, I need assurance that everything is okay, meaning that in order for me to hear her voice and not the voice of my own internal dialogue, I need to know the end of the story at the beginning. Then she can go back and fill in the details. The other way drives me nuts! It is also important to note that as much as I need to know that everything is okay, DeeDee needs to communicate the details. Make sure you give your wife the gift of listening completely to whatever she is communicating.

You and your spouse must agree to communicate honestly and openly. Even though I am brutally honest, that is not an excuse to be blunt and hurtful to DeeDee; neither is it an excuse for you to be hurtful to your spouse. There are some areas you can discuss straight on with your spouse and other areas that you must be more considerate and strategic, areas where your spouse is tender or vulnerable. With DeeDee, I know that I can discuss ministry straight on. When discussing the children and how they are raised, I must be gentler. How she looks – tender; how the car is running - straight on. Be sensitive to each other's needs and feelings and learn to respect each other's views, even if they differ. Proverbs 4:7 says, "**Wisdom** is the principal thing; therefore get **wisdom**: and with all thy getting get understanding." (emphasis mine)

Just like our God, we are speaking spirits. We have today what we spoke of yesterday. Often we don't connect our words to our results because of the time factor between when we sow the words and when we reap the harvest of our sowing those words. Can you imagine what would happen if everything we said came to pass immediately? "'I laughed myself to death" and immediately you dropped dead. "You make me sick" and instantly, you were sick. If it happened like that, we would definitely be more careful about our words. Since it doesn't happen that quickly, we tend to be sloppy and lazy with our language. Know this, what you say happens just the way you say it, the manifestation is just delayed. Why not use that energy to state the positive things you want to see in your life rather than perpetuating the negativity?

Speaking is not the only way we communicate. As a matter of fact, it's been reported that only 7 percent of communication is verbal. Thirty-eight percent is vocal meaning volume, pitch and rhythm, and 55 percent is our body language - mostly facial expressions. Even when your mouth is not open, you are still communicating something. These statistics indicate that learning to communicate non-verbally is as important as learning to speak. There's nothing worse than saying with your words that the family finances are fine and then shrugging your shoulders, frowning and walking away from your spouse. You are sending a mixed message which creates confusion. There must be congruence in your verbal and non-verbal communication with your spouse. Be mindful of what your actions and expressions communicate when you're having a discussion. Conversely, non-verbal communication is a great way to make your spouse feel loved. Grab her hand, put your arm around her shoulder. As a matter of fact, recent research shows that hugging someone has a positive, calming effect on both people. Hug each other – right now.

If something your husband said hurt your feelings, let him know that you are hurting. If something your wife did made you feel ignored or unimportant, it is imperative that you communicate it so the issue can be addressed. Passive-aggressive mind games and the silent treatment are ineffective ways of communicating your true feelings. We're all adults here, so it's time to speak up and stand up for a better marriage – and it begins with making open and honest communication a priority in your marriage.

So, when you don't understand something, instead of responding in a manner that may make matters worse, ask clarifying questions to ensure you understand exactly what is being conveyed. This will certainly require patience on the part of the speaker. In the event that the listener isn't clear on what the speaker has said and is requesting clarity, the speaker must be loving enough to take the time to accommodate the listener. That may mean saying the same thing more than once, in different ways, using a different tone, to make sure you are being understood, that your signal is being received properly, and you're doing it in a manner that ministers grace to the hearer. Your ability to communicate effectively will determine whether you build up or tear down your marriage. Proverbs 6:2

states, "Thou art snared with the words of thy mouth, thou art taken with the words of thy mouth." So, be careful what you say and be careful how you say it; even be careful of how you receive the communication of your spouse. Remember, your response is your responsibility. Again, this is work, but it is worth the work, so that God may be glorified, and you can have a *Marriage Made EZ.*

Scriptures (KJV)

Mark 11:23 "For verily I say unto you, That whosoever shall say unto this mountain, Be thou removed, and be thou cast into the sea; and shall not doubt in his heart, but shall believe that those things which he saith shall come to pass; he shall have whatsoever he saith."

James 1:5 "If any of you lack wisdom, let him ask of God, that giveth to all men liberally, and upbraideth not; and it shall be given him."

James 1:19 "Wherefore, my beloved brethren, let every man be swift to hear, slow to speak, slow to wrath."

Scriptures (MSG)

Proverbs 18:21 "Words kill, words give life; they're either poison or fruit—you choose."

Exercises

Make a list of topics to discuss with your spouse. Which ones can you discuss straight on, and which ones must you be more strategic? Share the list with your spouse to see if your assessment is accurate. Discuss your answers openly.

Communication can be verbal or non-verbal and includes body language. Sit down together and make faces, and tell your mate what that facial expression means to you. Fold your arms or turn away from each other – how does that make you feel? What is being conveyed? Discuss words and statements that you do not like and make them a part of a list of words that will never be used again. Also, discuss words and statements that you like to hear from your spouse. Maybe even create "fun" consequences for using those words. Honoring your mate's request is vitally important to improving your communication.

Be sure to record your findings on the following pages.

Confession

I walk in agreement with my spouse as we enjoy careful communication with one another. I use the power of my words to build him/her up in our faith. I only speak words of life that inspire, improve and increase my spouse.

How do you agree on everything and respect each other's views even if they are different?

Tasha Work on non verbal Communication, Volume, pitch & rhythm.

DAY 6:

COMMUNICATION - LISTENING vs. HEARING

Since we started the discussion of communication yesterday, I thought it would be good to fortify our time of communicating by putting emphasis on two areas that are imperative to effective communication: hearing and listening. As children, we were taught how to speak and how to hear; all of our parents asked us repeatedly, "Did you hear me?" We were taught to hear but never taught how to listen effectively. As we grew up, our speaking skills were continually sharpened as our parents corrected our subject-verb disagreements, and we participated in spelling bees. Yet rarely, if ever, have we been taught how to listen, and listening is absolutely essential in communicating. It's just like sowing and reaping. You cannot have any reaping without sowing and you can't have any sowing without reaping. The minute one or the other ceases, the entire system fails. In like fashion, you cannot have clear communication without effective listening.

Truly there is a difference between hearing and listening. Please don't get them confused. Hearing is simply the ability to perceive sounds. It is only when we hear with the intention of understanding that it can be considered listening – the true art of fully engaging. Listening is about hearing for understanding.

It is giving 100 percent of your attention to what is being said, not thinking about what your response is going to be and definitely not cutting the speaker off mid-sentence which, by the way, is a blatant sign of disrespect. As a matter of fact, in some cultures, cutting someone off midsentence is punishable by death! Okay, not physical death, but the death of your relationship.

Think of how often you just want someone to listen to you - not to solve your problem, but just to listen as you give them a complete picture of what you are experiencing and therefore attempting to communicate. I am not saying that anyone should be allowed to dump on you or just say anything they want to you. I'm talking about showing how much we care by slowing down to hear our spouse completely. One of the greatest gifts we give our loved ones is being a good listener. If we listen better, we can respond more accurately. If we respond more accurately, we eliminate more disagreements, differences, debates, and disasters.

In our journey to a *Marriage Made EZ,* I learned that even when you hear wrong and/or it's said wrong, as I shared on Day 4, your response is still your responsibility. People often say things like, "I wouldn't have said this or that or acted that way if you hadn't said what you said or done what you did." Basically they are attempting to relinquish their responsibility onto someone else and, in essence, are giving up their personal power to the very person they are upset with. They didn't MAKE you mad. They presented an opportunity to be mad and you seized it. You could have chosen not to be mad just like you chose to be mad. Again, your response is your responsibility.

James 1:19 (AMP) says, "Understand [this], my beloved brethren. Let every man be quick to hear [a ready listener], slow to speak, slow to take offense and to get angry. Be a ready listener and a slow speaker. "

Proverbs 18:13 (MSG) says, "Answering before listening is both stupid and rude." *Stupid and rude* are adjectives that we would never want anyone to use to describe us. The bottom line is that it is a foolish man who answers a matter before it has been fully heard. Giving your mate the benefit of the doubt in things that are said is critical. In the past, DeeDee would say certain things a certain way and I would react negatively. One day she abruptly stopped me and asked, "If you know I love you, why would you think I would attack you?" Just the way she said things would cause me to think something different than what she stated. I had to learn to take into consideration her heart towards me and allow that to guide me in responding to her rather than getting in the flesh to correct her in a way that would cause more confusion.

Think about this: our success in having a good relationship with Jesus Christ relies heavily on our ability to listen and obey His voice. John 10:27 (AMP) says, "The sheep that are my own hear and are listening to my voice; and I know them, and they follow Me." Imagine not hearing, listening, and obeying the voice of God. God told Joshua to march around the Jericho wall seven times. What if Joshua thought he heard to march only six times? The walls wouldn't have come down. If the prophet of God told Naaman to dip in the pool seven times and he only dipped six times, then he would have died a leper. Hearing and listening are vitally important in your relationship. Decide today to listen completely to your spouse.

Even still, there are times when you may have to adjust your strategy. Try writing a letter or recording a voice mail message and be absent when your spouse reads or listens to it. This will

give him/her time to completely hear what it is you are attempting to communicate without feeling the pressure of having to respond. When you are the listening or reading spouse, be sure to seek God for full understanding of your spouse's issue before delivering your response.

Scriptures (KJV)

Luke 8:18	"Take heed therefore ***how*** you hear: for whosoever hath, to him shall be given; and whosoever hath not, from him shall be taken even that which he seemeth to have." [emphasis added]
Revelations 3:22	"He that hath an ear, let him hear what the Spirit saith unto the churches."

Scriptures (AMP)

Mark 4:24	"And He said to them, Be careful what you are hearing. The measure [of thought and study] you give [to the truth you hear] will be the measure [of virtue and knowledge] that comes back to you—and more [besides]will be given to you who hear."

Scriptures (MSG)

John 10:27-30	"My sheep recognize my voice. I know them, and they follow me. I give them real and eternal life. They are protected from the Destroyer for good. No one can steal them from out of my hand. The Father who put them under my care is so much greater than the Destroyer and Thief. No one could

	ever get them away from him. I and the Father are one heart and mind."
James 1:19-21	"Post this at all the intersections, dear friends: Lead with your ears, follow up with your tongue, and let anger straggle along in the rear. God's righteousness doesn't grow from human anger. So throw all spoiled virtue and cancerous evil in the garbage. In simple humility, let our gardener, God, landscape you with the Word, making a salvation-garden of your life."

Exercise

Practice listening to each other. Write a letter to vocalize thoughts and feelings that you have not been able to effectively communicate in the past. Each spouse should be given the opportunity to read his/her letter uninterrupted. After the first letter is read, don't jump to any conclusions. Take time to ask questions and understand what was said. Then repeat the exercise for the other spouse. Record your discovery on the following pages.

Confession

I listen carefully to not only my spouse's words, but to his/her heart, and I respond appropriately. (Say it to yourself and to each other.)

____

____

____

DAY 7:

COMMUNICATION - THINK BEFORE YOU SPEAK

As we continue our conversation regarding communication, we must address the power of our thoughts and their role in what we say and do. If you want to change your situation, then you must first change your thinking about the situation. Every action and every impulse starts with a thought. Then we meditate on that thought, and it becomes an action. Those repeated actions become habits, and those habits develop the character of who we are.

God does not send you self-defeating thoughts. For some reason, this is a foreign concept to most of us. We don't seem to accept that in our marriages, and instead, we meditate on the thoughts that are designed to defeat us. We think negative things about our spouses and about our relationship and then wonder why our marriage seems to be deteriorating into an unhappy, negative, and miserable rut. It's because you've allowed negative thoughts and actions to prevail. Focus on thinking only on the promise and provision, not the problem.

Beware of the devil's devices. Once he starts to control your thinking, then he can control your decisions and, ultimately, your mind. Be careful about the advice of unmarried people or people who have been unsuccessful at marriage. It's amazing how many of us make decisions based on someone else's failures and expect to succeed as a result. When you let them get into your thinking, then you give them access and power over your relationship with your spouse and we all have heard the story of the former best friend dating their friend's husband.

"And be not conformed to this world: but be ye transformed by the renewing of your mind, that ye may prove what [is] that good, and acceptable, and perfect, Will of God" (Romans 12:2, KJV). The Message Bible shares this translation: "So here's what I want you to do, God helping you: Take your everyday, ordinary life—your sleeping, eating, going-to-work, and walking-around life—and place it before God as an offering. Embracing what God does for you is the best thing you can do for him. Don't become so well-adjusted to your culture that you fit into it without even thinking. Instead, fix your attention on God. You'll be changed from the inside out. Readily recognize what he wants from you, and quickly respond to it. Unlike the culture around you, always dragging you down to its level of immaturity, God brings the best out of you, develops well-formed maturity in you." (Romans 12:1-2, MSG)

Give your marriage and its problems to God. Allow the Spirit of God to govern your thoughts. Trying to figure it out in your head brings doubt in your heart. Where there is doubt, there is fear. Where there is fear, there is failure. Since God has not given us the spirit of fear, it is not His will that we should be fearful or experience failure in the things that He has promised. God wants your marriage to succeed.

How do you control your thoughts? I'm sure glad you asked that. Start with changing your focus. What you focus on expands, good or bad. If you want more love, focus on ways to build on the love that you have. Focus will help you to stay <u>*F*</u>irmly <u>*O*</u>n <u>*C*</u>ourse <u>*U*</u>ntil <u>*S*</u>uccessful.

Additionally, we must be aware of what we say. We've all heard it said that "sticks and stones may break my bones, but words will never hurt me." How untrue. Yet we allow our kids to grow up thinking that the spoken word carries no weight, and as a result, they use language lazily. I remember DeeDee doing an exercise with our children to teach them how powerful words are. She took them outside to blow bubbles. Once they had blown the bubbles, she told them to catch the bubbles and put them back into the bottle. Of course, they weren't able to catch them. DeeDee told them that the bubbles were like words. Once you've put the words out there, it's impossible to get them back. How much more relevant is that statement to those of us who are married? Put a watch over your mouth and only speak those things which will bring edification and growth to your spouse.

<u>**Scriptures (KJV)**</u>

Luke 6:45	"A good man out of the good treasure of his heart bringeth forth that which is good; and an evil man out of the evil treasure of his heart bringeth forth that which is evil: for of the abundance of the heart his mouth speaketh."
Psalms 119:11	"Thy word have I hid in mine heart, that I might not sin against thee."
Proverbs 23:7a	"For as he thinketh in his heart, so is he:"

Scriptures (AMP)

Prov. 10:19	"In the multitude of words there wanteth not sin: but he that refraineth his lips is wise."

Scriptures (MSG)

Matthew 12:34-37	"You have minds like a snake pit! How do you suppose what you say is worth anything when you are so foul-minded? It's your heart, not the dictionary that gives meaning to your words. A good person produces good deeds and words season after season. An evil person is a blight on the orchard. Let me tell you something: Every one of these careless words is going to come back to haunt you. There will be a time of Reckoning. Words are powerful; take them seriously. Words can be your salvation. Words can also be your damnation."

Exercise

Pay attention to the type of information that you encounter throughout the course of a day - the amount of negative and toxic messages you receive through music, videos, and television broadcasts. Adjust the level of negative information you absorb and counteract it by watching your *Marriage Made EZ* DVD or broadcast or listen to a *Marriage Made EZ* CD. Meditate on the Scriptures that I've given you through this book while you make plans to attend a live *Marriage Made EZ* event. We would love to meet you and your spouse there.

For 10 minutes, listen to your spouse as they speak. No interrupting, no glazed eyes. Stay focused on every word and emotion your spouse is conveying. Switch. Now discuss whether or not that was easy. Be transparent. We're growing and developing into excellent communicators!

What did you learn in this exercise? Be sure to note those key points on the following pages.

Confession

Thy word have I hid in mine heart that I might not sin against thee. I will meditate on good things and good thoughts, because my thoughts direct my actions.

DAY 8:

IF YOU MUST DISAGREE, DO SO AGREEABLY

It amazes me how few people really understand the underlying reasons for arguing. Outside of trying to change someone's mind or opinion about something, I have not found any reason to argue. Often, we find ourselves arguing over something that they, as an adult, have a right to – whether it is a belief or a desire. So arguing is really about disrespect, control, and getting your own way. You are pretty much telling the other person that they don't have a right to their own thinking or they aren't smart enough to make the decision for themselves. In either case, there is no winning.

Read the Word of God and you will realize that you never have to argue again. A husband's obligation is to love his wife as Christ loved the church. Can you imagine Jesus yelling or screaming at the church – or calling her anything other than her name? Of course not! As Christians, we are not just believers in Christ, we are followers of Christ. That means our behavior should model His example as set forth in His Word.

Never arguing doesn't mean never disagreeing. It means that as a couple, you find a reasonable and respectful way to voice your concerns without harming or violating your spouse's right to feel differently about a particular issue. To take this a step

further, not only can you completely avoid arguing – you can always agree. (The Father, Son, and Holy Spirit are in such perfect agreement, they are ONE.) Instead of focusing on how you feel and what you want, focus on what God says and what He wills. A couple in Christ that commits to always seeking God's Will first will rarely, if ever, experience arguments and disagreements. Marriage is a covenant of agreement and oneness before God. Amos 3:3 says, "How can two walk together except they be agreed?" You cannot walk with God if you don't agree. To walk with God together, you must be in agreement as husband and wife.

The Bible states that love keeps no record of wrong doing. This means we have to fix the way we deal with disagreements, so that we can bounce back and not harbor resentment about them. Changing the way you deal with disagreement transforms your relationship, but in order to do that, you must first transform your thinking.

Micah 7:18 in the Message Bible says, "Don't nurse your anger and don't stay angry long, for mercy is your specialty." By holding on to disagreement, you are going to let it destroy you and ruin your relationship. Just as we discussed on Day 4, we are responsible for our actions, and we must live in an excuse-free zone; we can't make them and we can't take them. Even when you think your wife is wrong, I believe it is still the husband's responsibility to go to the wife to begin the process of reconciliation. It may mean getting your feelings hurt, it may mean feeling lesser than, but the Bible states 'The greater one is going to be least among you." Humble yourself and let your spouse know that they are worth the fight. The marriage covenant is serious and it's not enough for you to just "exist" with one another.

Since most of us can hardly conceive of a marriage without arguments and disagreements, let's talk about how to disagree agreeably. That means no dirty tricks, no mind games and no below-the-belt punches. When two people are involved, inevitably there will be situations where confrontation is necessary. It is important to note that confrontation is for restoration and reconciliation, not to destroy or tear each other down. At points of turmoil or disagreement in your marriage, remember to think on the promise and provision, not the problem. Take God at His Word, knowing that you will get through this moment of discord. Stagger not. It is your duty to be fully persuaded that God is "able (and willing) to do exceeding, abundantly, above all that we ask or think according to the power that works in us." (Ephesians 3:20, KJV)

A well-known televangelist who has been married for more than 40 years once said that he and his wife developed a 1 to 10 "Richter scale" for disagreements in their marriage to determine how intense their fellowship should be to resolve an issue. Basically, a 1 on the scale translates to "I don't agree with what you're saying, but the impact is minor, so you can do what you want." A 5 on the scale equates to, "I disagree with your point of view. I do not support this course of action and we need to discuss this until we can find common ground and make a decision we're both comfortable with." A 10 on the scale means, "Over my dead body!!! I absolutely do not support this decision and I will not stand for it. We will not move forward until this is resolved. We need to pray about this now!" One couple at our *Marriage Made EZ* event mentioned that they use rock, stone, and cinderblock to communicate pending disagreement. When one spouse responds "rock" to something the other spouse says, they know that they're beginning to agitate them. If they say "boulder," they know they need to back off and let the other spouse calm down before continuing the conversation. If they say "cinderblock," it's on and you may even need to begin reconciliatory means to maintain fellowship with your spouse. Still another couple mentioned that just like in football when the referee throws up his flag in reference to a penalty, when he/she says or does something offensive, they simply say or throw a "flag on the play." The great thing about either of these systems is that no matter where you fall on the scale, it forces you to communicate and talk through what you're thinking and feeling. Communication and praying together will work wonders for any level of disagreement in a marriage.

Make a conscious agreement to retreat and assess the situation when there is disagreement between you. The key is finding some place of agreement. So agree that each spouse will go to God, on their own, and return calmer, clearer, and with the answers they have received from the throne of grace. God is no respecter of persons and He will have the same conversation with each spouse in a way that they can receive it. Often, they will be able to receive an answer from Him before they can receive from each other. And, when they come back together to talk, there is unity and the power of agreement working to bridge the gap in their communication.

I can't tell you how many times DeeDee and I have experienced this phenomenon. On Sunday mornings, DeeDee and I normally attend three separate worship services together. This particular Sunday morning, I was thinking of asking her to attend our Ellicott City location while I attended a different service. Before I could even bring the conversation up, she asked me, "Did you want me to go to E-City?" Because we serve the same God, He had given us the same message and had already prepared her to be open to my request. No strife. No strain. No struggle. No stress. *Marriage Made EZ.*

The next time you are about to get into intense fellowship on a matter, STOP. Take a moment to reflect and ask the following question aloud: "How does God want us to handle this situation?"

Scriptures (AMP)

John 16:33 "I have told you these things, so that in Me you may have [perfect] peace and confidence. In the world you have tribulation and trials and distress and frustration; but be of good cheer [take courage; be confident, certain, undaunted]! For I have overcome the world. [I have deprived it of power to harm you and have conquered it for you.]"

John 14:27 "Peace I leave with you, My [own] peace I now give and bequeath to you. Not as the world gives do I give to you. Do not let your hearts be troubled, neither let them be afraid. [Stop allowing yourselves to be agitated and disturbed; and do not permit yourselves to be fearful and intimidated and cowardly and unsettled.]"

Hebrews 4:16 "Let us then fearlessly and confidently and boldly draw near to the throne of grace (the throne of God's unmerited favor to us sinners), that we may receive mercy [for our failures] and find grace to help in good time for every need [appropriate help and well-timed help, coming just when we need it]."

Exercise

Create a system for you and your spouse to recognize when a disagreement is moving into an argument or intense fellowship. Maybe use a system like we mentioned earlier in this section,

the "Richter" scale or something else. Maybe it's as simple as throwing a "flag on the play." Whatever it is you should both recognize that you're treading on dangerous ground. Remember, we are in ministry to one another and we are not there to add drama and trauma to each other's life.

Confession

I agreeably deal with the intense fellowship in my marriage knowing that with the power that lives in me, I have grace, mercy, peace and patience in the midst of every storm.

DAY 9:

UNITY - THE POWER OF AGREEMENT

Let's talk more about our statement from yesterday: the Father, Son, and Holy Spirit are in such agreement that they are ONE. Can you say that about you and your spouse? Do you share common vision, purpose, goals, and focus in your marriage? How would you describe your decision-making process? How does your level of agreement measure up? We're told in Matthew 18:19, "That if any two agree on earth as touching anything that they shall ask, it shall be done for them of the Father in heaven to glorify His Son Jesus." Power is released when you agree, which you have no access to when you disagree.

Agreement in your marriage is defined as the coming together of you and your spouse to form like-mindedness and harmony on any one thing. God is a great conductor and He designed a man and woman in marriage to harmonize – like a well-rehearsed symphony. Although there are different instruments and different notes, when they come together in unity, the musicians all play the same melody. That's how life and marriage were originally designed to be and that's how they can be again if you're willing to mutually submit to one another and allow God to conduct your marriage.

Remember, there is strength in unity and power in agreement. Unity and agreement are biblical principles which means they work regardless of who uses them and regardless of their belief systems. Think about the Tower of Babel in the book of Genesis (referenced in Day 5) and how their united focus allowed them to come together as one to build a tower into the heavens. God realized that the unity of the people would allow them to accomplish anything: good, bad, or ugly. The same is true now. Also, think about the amount of power that was present on the day of Pentecost when the saints of God were all functioning in one accord. That very same power is available to you today.

The power of agreement is another benefit to your marriage covenant. The Bible says that one can chase a thousand and two can chase 10,000. Amos 3:3 says, "How can two walk together lest they be agreed." The key to unity is *U-N-I* (you in I) and *I-N-U* (I in you). The key to unity in marriage is found in Psalms 133:1 which reads, "Behold, how good and how pleasant it is for brethren to dwell together in unity!" For a husband and his wife, an understanding of unity is a crucial key to *Marriage Made EZ.* The concept of unity is adopting an attitude and mindset that the two individuals, becoming one, is about total unity: U-N-I (you in I) and I-N-U (I in you). It is about functioning with U-N-IT (you in it) fully, with no back doors or escape hatches. Once you become a UNIT all that is left is the Y (why). Why? UNITY is what was in the mind of God from the very beginning. Even as you read Psalms 133:3, you find that the place of blessing is where there is unity.

Unity is the foundation necessary to protect each other and to keep each other's secrets. The last thing your spouse wants to hear is his/her secrets from someone else. Some information between couples should remain just between the couple, no matter how close or open you are with other family members and friends. Even the justice system in the United States makes allowances for husbands and wives to maintain one another's confidentiality in that the law gives spouses immunity from testifying against one another. There's something unique and significant about the bond of intimacy formed by mutual secrecy within a marriage - information and intimate knowledge that no one else is privy to. Your marriage should have its own "secret language" or "secret access code" and no one else should be allowed in.

Scriptures (MSG)

Psalms 133:1 "How wonderful, how beautiful, when brothers and sisters get along!"

Phil. 2:1-4 "If you've gotten anything at all out of following Christ, if his love has made any difference in your life, if being in a community of the Spirit means anything to you, if you have a heart, if you care—then do me a favor: Agree with each other, love each other, be deep-spirited friends. Don't push your way to the front; don't sweet-talk your way to the top. Put yourself aside, and help others get ahead. Don't be obsessed with getting your own advantage. Forget yourselves long enough to lend a helping hand."

Scriptures (AMP)

Eccl. 4:12 "And though a man might prevail against him who is alone, two will withstand him. A threefold cord is not quickly broken."

Scriptures (KJV)

Matt. 18:19 "Again I say unto you, That if two of you shall agree on earth as touching anything that they shall ask, it shall be done for them of my Father which is in heaven."

Acts 2:1 "And when the day of Pentecost was fully come, they were all with one accord in one place."

Exercise

Today, practice staying in agreement with your spouse. Pray together and ask that God, by His Spirit, would strengthen your marriage through the power of agreement. Work to make this a daily practice in your lives. Also, what can you join together, in faith, to believe God for, maybe money for a house, a special vacation or even to go out to dinner. Be sure to note on the following pages your insights and experiences from the day.

Confession

We walk in the power of agreement and as such, anything that we ask shall be done for us from our Father which is in heaven.

____

____

____

____

____

____

____

DAY 10:
WRITE YOUR VISION

We are so bombarded with images about marriage from the media and the world that we've lost focus on marriage's true meaning and why God created it. Marriage is God's demonstration and reflection of the love Christ has for the church and thus our marriage should reflect that. To create a new vision for your marriage, you will have to use the Word of God to develop a mental image and disposition of how you want your marriage to be and what you want it to represent. Your marriage must be greater than you – it must be a representation of something greater than you, a representation of Christ. By using the Word of God, you and your marriage will become more Christ-centered and fruitful and move away from being self-centered. We use the Word of God to accomplish material things, so why not use the Word to accomplish God's vision for our marriage?

This vision is not based on emotions, but on God's Word. God knows the purpose and rewards of marriage. Ecclesiastes 4:9-12 says, "Two are better than one because they have a good reward for their labor ... and a threefold cord is not easily broken." God spoke marriage into existence and had a need and a plan for it. The enemy knows of this plan which is why he diligently tries to cause division, discord, and divorce, because it disrupts the plan and purpose of God. Understand that the quality of your relationship will be tested, and if the proper foundation is not in place, then your marriage is built on sand and it will not withstand a storm. Use the principles of the Word of God and cause your relationship to go to the next level, to reflect His nature and to fulfill His plan for your life. While you are creating this vision for your marriage, you must program your mind to filter out anything that goes against that vision. The Word will also act as a filter, causing you not to focus on the negatives. The best way to predict the future of your marriage is to create it yourself. My marriage to DeeDee has been changed as a result of our having a shared vision. Proverbs 29:18 states, "Where there is no vision, the people perish." (KJV) God uses vision to get us to the next level, as well as to bring about restraint. Vision allows you to see beyond your present circumstances and into the greatness that God has ordained for your marriage relationship. Pastor Yonggi Cho, pastor of the largest church in Seoul Korea, attributes all that he has accomplished to his God-breathed vision, his faith, and his speaking the vision consistently. Again, God is a God of order and there is an order in obtaining everything we want in life.

We are created with a purpose and infused with vision. Our journey in life is about defining and clarifying God's original intent for creating us, which is to get clear on God's vision for our marriages and for our lives. God is no respecter of persons; what He has done for one, He will do for another if they exercise the same principles in faith. Simply put, you can have everything DeeDee and I have if you're willing to exercise the same principles and level of faith we did to get it. Get clear on God's vision for your life. If you can see it, you can seize it. Simply work the Word. Habakkuk 2:2 declares, "Write the vision down. Make it plain upon tables so that everyone who reads it can run with it." Be steadfast and unmovable and build relationships with people of similar vision.

Vision provides direction and purpose. Vision will also add meaning to your life and marriage. Vision challenges us to press forward and to hold our course. It is important that you know what I call the 4Ps of vision: the Power of vision, the Purpose of vision, the Price of vision, and the Payoff of vision. ***Your vision has POWER to complete your PURPOSE and if you're willing to pay the PRICE there is a great PAYOFF for you and your family for generations to come.***

Once we see the vision, it's time to start seizing the vision. Tomorrow is not promised to any of us. We must begin right now. See yourself firmly planted in your vision doing your God-ordained purpose. Envision your tomorrows being brighter than your yesterdays. This is precisely how we have attained success in our marriage.

It's been my observation that most couples have never even sat down to write the vision for their marriage. The husband, in most cases, should be equipped with the vision and it should be agreed upon by the wife. Where do you want to be in 1 to 5 years? What do you want to accomplish both individually and as a couple? Are you going to build a new home? Are you going to start a new business? Will you have more children? Will you embark upon a ministry venture? Are you planning to be happy together? It is time for you to come together to put these plans into action, so that they become a reality.

Romans 2:11 explains that there is no respect of persons with God. He is a respecter of vision and faith. God uses people to accomplish His Will in the earth. Remember, God plans and man plans; God's plan is always better. Abraham had vision and Moses had vision; Joshua, Isaiah, Paul, and Jesus himself had

vision. Mike Freeman also has a vision for the future of your marriage and what I see and speak comes to pass.

> ***"I see this information catapulting your marriage into new dimensions of faith, power, and authority. You have the book in your hand because you have the ability in your heart. Every good thing that I have in my marriage, I release into yours NOW, in Jesus' name."***

Just as I have clearly communicated my vision for your marriage so that there is no misunderstanding, we must communicate vision to our spouses. Don't assume they are aware of what you are trying to accomplish.

There is a systematic way of seeing your vision come into fruition. Simply say it, see it, believe it, and achieve it. Systems are designed to function as such, that they take no account of who you are, what your background is, or even where you come from. Anyone can plug into the system that someone else has used and get the same results. You will <u>*S*</u>ave <u>*Y*</u>ourself *S*ome <u>*T*</u>ime <u>*E*</u>nergy and <u>*M*</u>oney if you will learn to identify and use the systems that God has already put in place. Think about it. God is totally systematic. Everything that He has created functions systemically; there is order to everything that He put in place. There's the solar system, respiratory system, circulatory system, muscular system, and many more. Systems give you specific, predetermined results, so if you want a specific outcome, participate in the system that creates it.

Vision will also help you to protect your focus, predict your friends, preserve your faith, paralyze fear, promote fortitude and pursue your future. Vision will keep you excited and provide a mental image that is produced by your imagination and infused by the Holy Spirit. This will in turn create habits and routines that will push you toward your desired result. Get your vision in your heart and keep it there. Whatever is in your heart will reflect in your attitude. Don't allow frustrations to cause you to be sidetracked from your vision. Hold your course, and it shall come to pass.

Psalm 45:1 proclaims, "My tongue is as the pen of a ready writer." When you speak in faith regarding what you want to come to pass, you will eventually see your vision come to life. Remember, we achieve our goals through vision, faith, and speaking: that which you do not want to see, don't give it life by talking about it. This is a principle that if you grasp it and apply it, all of your relationships will be changed and, therefore, it bears repeating. Start talking about what you DO want, and stop talking about what you DON'T want.

When DeeDee and I first got married, we knew that we didn't want to live in an apartment. From the very beginning we decided that we were going to own something, at least a townhome. However, we both had different ideas about spending money and that hindered our progress to home ownership. It was not until we came together to achieve the common goal of buying a home, that we agreed and refrained from frivolous spending and pooled our resources to bring our vision into fruition. The vision brought about restraints. It gave us something bigger than ourselves to focus our attention on. In this process, we implemented a four-step formula for achieving vision: Visualize it, Verbalize it, Internalize it, until you Materialize it. This is how you begin to live life from the inside-out, rather than the other way around. My prayer is that you begin to see what God intended for you to have from the very beginning of your relationship and work together to bring that vision to pass.

Scriptures (KJV)

Habakkuk 2:2	"And the Lord answered me, and said, Write the vision, and make it plain upon tables, that he may run that readeth it."
Proverbs 29:18a	"Where there is no vision, the people perish:"

Scriptures (MSG)

Habakkuk 2:3	"This vision-message is a witness pointing to what's coming. It aches for the coming—it can hardly wait! And it doesn't lie. If it seems slow in coming, wait. It's on its way. It will come right on time."
Acts 10:34-35	"Peter fairly exploded with his good news: It's God's own truth, nothing could be plainer: god plays no favorites! It makes no difference who you are or where you're from – if you want God and are ready to do as he says, the door is open. The Message he sent to the children of Israel – that through Jesus Christ everything is being put together again – well, he's doing it everywhere, among everyone."

Exercises

Sit down with your partner and write an outline of the vision for your marriage. (This written document should become part of your Family Constitution that we begin to develop on Day 12.)

Confession

Add what you wrote here as the vision for your marriage. Follow that with this confession:

"Because we have visualized it (see it), verbalized it (say it), internalized it (believe it) and are materializing it (achieve it), the written vision for our marriage and family will come to pass in Jesus' name."

DAY 11:

FAMILY MEETINGS
WE'RE IN THIS TOGETHER

One of the key events for our family has been our family meetings. We meet together as a couple and we also meet with our children as a family. Of course, what we share at our private meetings is different from the meetings with the entire family. Based on your family structure, you can determine how often you need to meet as a couple and how often you need to meet with the entire family. Your family structure should be decided and designed in a Family Meeting and then become part of your Family Constitution, which we will discuss tomorrow, Day 12.

As our children were growing up, every seven days we had a family meeting to discuss the progress made within a given time period. Family meetings are just like any other corporation or organization's meeting. They help to determine the progress and success of all of the parties that are involved. The whole is the sum total of all of its parts and in order for the whole to be whole, complete, focused and together, we must monitor how the parts are functioning.

Our family meetings are designed so that each person reports on what they have done. It's Judgment Day. It's Reckoning Day. It's time to give an account for what you have accomplished since our last meeting. If you were sitting in a boardroom and you were given an assignment to fulfill within a certain time period and you came back to the meeting without your assignments completed, you would be fined or fired. However, when you understand the importance of fulfilling your assignment and that it sustains your livelihood, you gladly hold up your end of the bargain. I want you to take this exchange seriously. I want you to come to your meetings prepared, having completed your assignments, so that you can be proud of the progress you have made. Just do it to advance your family.

Make sure there are guidelines and rules for your family meeting. For example, we designated an uninterrupted 55 minutes (never longer) for our meetings, scheduled at a time when there are no distractions. You all deserve each other's undivided attention. You want your spouse to know that they are a valuable entity and significant part of this organization. We want your relationship to be used as a trophy to show the world what God intended for marriage to look like from the very beginning.

Some families will have to grow into having effective family meetings. In this instance, effective means calm, without yelling or division. Until your relationship has grown to this place, you may have to strategically make adjustments to your meeting plan. Maybe you need to go to a public place to talk so no one acts out. Maybe you need to involve another Godly couple to assist in this guided conversation. Whatever you need to do to have effective family meetings, do it.

One of the funniest family meetings we ever had happened when our daughter Brittney was 12 or 13 years old and our son Josh was 9. A topic during the meeting was sex. We were beginning our discussion about their involvement, the importance of sex and what our expectation was as a family regarding sex. We asked the kids if any of them wanted to or did they know of any teenagers that were having sex. They flat out told us emphatically, yes! And Josh, with his vintage style of humor replied, "Come on Dad, do you know any 9-year-old that doesn't want to have sex these days?" His response was absolutely hilarious and we laughed and laughed, pretty much through the entire meeting. Just be aware, family meetings sometimes take a turn for the hilarious, just as they at times take a turn for more challenging.

One of our worst meetings took place when DeeDee was sharing a monthly report of the household expenses. It was obvious that DeeDee was reporting inaccurate information. The numbers were wrong, and it looked like we didn't have the amount of money she thought we did. It also appeared that it was going to create a tremendous strain on our relationship and the meeting and neither of us wanted that. We looked at each other and got completely silent, neither of us knowing what to do. I didn't want to discuss her screwing up the books and she was already so disappointed in herself that neither of us said anything at all. So what did we do? We stopped that conversation and moved on. With the knowledge that the family meeting was designed to establish unity and camaraderie, we didn't want to do anything to counteract that. Even with the challenge that was created, we didn't talk about it again until the next family meeting. At that meeting she gave another report, a more accurate one and we were able to move on.

Regardless of what is shared at your family meetings, be sure to maintain peace, calmness, and agreement with your spouse. These meetings will begin to shape how you interact with one another and will assist you in building a *Marriage Made EZ.*

Scriptures (KJV)

Genesis 12:2	"And I will make of thee a great nation, and I will bless thee, and make thy name great; and thou shalt be a blessing."
Proverbs 22:6	"Train up a child in the way he should go: and when he is old, he will not depart from it."
1 Corinthians 12:12	"For as the body is one, and hath many members, and all the members of that one body, being many, are one body, are so also is Christ."

Exercise

Schedule your first family meeting with your spouse. At this meeting, you should develop the roles and guidelines for your meetings. Agree that there will be no walking away, no interruptions, and no raised voices. Give it a definite start time and an end time - no more than 55 minutes. (Husbands, this is also your opportunity to schedule date night which should happen no less than every other week. You make all of the plans for you and your wife... only. Do not involve anyone else.)

Next, schedule a meeting for the entire family. All family members should be given an opportunity to share what's on their heart and mind, their visions and goals, what new activities or projects they're participating in at school or work. They should also share what they've accomplished in the past week so that, as a family, you can pray over them individually and collectively. Before adjourning, pray together as a family and schedule the next meeting time.

Confession

Thank you, Father, that my marriage and my family are comforted knowing clearly our collective visions and expectations as a family and that I diligently seek to define them.

DAY 12:

FAMILY CONSTITUTION

Every organization (and family) should have a constitution, a document outlining the fundamental principles that prescribe the nature, function, and limits of an institution. Your family is no different. There are guidelines, rules, and regulations for every aspect of life. You can't function without them. The church, the workplace, school, the court system, and even our homes should have guidelines. The Word of God is the Constitution for the believer. When you and I accepted Jesus, we forfeited the right to do life on our own terms. We were given guidelines and a rule book to follow to make sure we conduct ourselves in a manner that pleases God. I liken this to growing up in your parents' home. Those who were raised in a home where there were rules and guidelines, understood that there was a definitive price to pay for noncompliance, trouble. Most of us remember the streetlight rule. When those lights came on, we had better be in the house or else! Need I say more? Rules were designed to ensure that everything would function decently and in order. Again, I can't overstate the fact that our God is a God of order. Please understand: to have a *Marriage Made EZ,* there must be order, a constitution and guidelines set forth whereby the union is governed and maintained.

DeeDee and I were able to make our marriage easy by establishing the Freeman Family Constitution. Why was this necessary? Because the power to define is the power to fulfill. Too many family members who are under our leadership are wandering generalities with no purpose and no direction. The Constitution creates boundaries and an understanding of who plays what role and who has what responsibility in our family. Within the Constitution are several rules of engagement. One of our most important rules is "Everyone knows where everyone goes." I can't get up and leave the house anytime I want to without informing someone where I am going and when I plan to return. We also had the "$100 rule." That rule states that expenses over $100 need to be agreed upon by both individuals. Of course, today, that cash amount has increased, but we still inform each other of our spending. We even have a rule concerning making the bed. That rule states that the last one out of bed makes it up. The Freeman Family Constitution has shaped how we function in our relationship. The values that we have may or may not work for your home, but get some in place now. Your next family meeting should include them.

One day, DeeDee and I were playing basketball. During the game, she didn't dribble the ball; she just picked it up and ran with it. (I didn't mind too much because I enjoyed checking her, if you know what I mean.) In any case, she started running off of the court, under the swing set and under the monkey bars. I became frustrated and refused to play. When she asked why I didn't want to play, I explained to her that the game was designed to be played within the boundaries (the white lines) of the court and because she wasn't adhering to the guidelines and the rules, if you will, I no longer wanted to play.

Years later I received a rhema word concerning that ill-fated basketball game. God showed me that just as I refused to play because DeeDee would not follow the rules of the game, He refuses to play if we live our lives outside of the boundaries He has set forth in His Word. He is not obligated to participate. Nothing will function properly without rules and guidelines. Today, I am asking you to establish guidelines regarding the rearing of your children, spending money, accountability, talking to each other and so on. How about considering never arguing again as one of the guidelines you establish in your marriage?

Joshua 24:15 says, "As for me and my house, we will serve the Lord." That declaration was for the entire house. Abraham's family was blessed because He assured God that he would govern his family according to the guidelines prescribed in His Word and, as a result, Abraham was called a friend of God. The Bible says the steps of a good man are ordered by the Lord. If you plan to get your marriage in order you must set forth rules and guidelines.

Additionally, some of these guidelines will have to be communicated to the rest of your family. Your Family Meeting is the place to communicate your Vision and Constitution to the rest of your household, as we discussed yesterday.

Scriptures (KJV)

Psalms 119:11	"Thy word have I hid in mine heart, that I might not sin against thee."
Joshua 1:8	"This book of the law shall not depart out of thy mouth; but thou shalt meditate therein day and night, that thou mayest observe to do according to all that is written therein: for then thou shalt make thy way prosperous, and then thou shalt have good success."

Hebrews 2:1 "Therefore we ought to give the more earnest heed to the things which we have heard, lest at any time we should let them slip."

Exercises

Come up with three guidelines you both can agree on. For example, some husbands have friends that their wives don't like and some wives have friends that their husbands don't like. Establish a guideline for friends and for the number of hours you work each week. Establish guidelines for discussions/disagreements. I don't know what is best for your particular relationship and I don't want to overwhelm you with a laundry list of things to do. Just start by setting three guidelines in place and working from there.

Together, plan and write a Family Constitution that outlines the "Rules of Order" for your family. Address issues such as finances, child rearing and discipline, how to handle disagreements, and where to spend special holidays with in-laws and family. This is an ongoing work in process. Be sure to include your guidelines on the following pages.

Confession

We commit to establish and adhere to Godly order and guidelines in our home. As for me and my house, we shall serve the Lord. (Joshua 24:15, KJV)

____

____

____

DAY 13:

BE HAPPY!

Wouldn't it be nice if husbands and wives could just relax and enjoy being with each other? Imagine for a moment how you would feel without the burden of worry; anxiety about bills and debt; concern about making ends meet; frustration about meeting the expectations of others, etc. How many people do you know who are actually happy? It seems that most people are just surviving and existing day-to-day in the same, dull routine of life. But the Word says that Jesus came to give us LIFE – and that more abundantly. We should have the expectation of a full, abundant, happy life. That's not to say there will not be trials, challenges, and difficult storms to endure; however, we have an intercessor in the form of the Holy Spirit who is interceding for us daily and guiding us down a path of fullness and joy.

Psalm 144:15 confirms that "Happy are the people whose God is the Lord!"

The people of God should be happy. We serve the King of Kings and Lord of Lords. We have direct access to the throne room of God and the guarantee of eternal life and peace in heaven for eternity through Christ. If that's not enough to be happy about, I don't know what is. The challenge comes in when we allow ourselves to get weighted down by the mundane tasks and responsibilities of life. God has told us clearly to cast our cares on Him because He cares for us. When we cast our cares on the Creator, we relinquish the need to carry our own burdens.

What if you just woke up one morning and had nothing to worry about? How would you spend the day? I know that seems like a far-fetched fantasy, and ironically, the truth is that so many people are so miserable, they don't even know how to be happy. Do you know what makes you happy? Do you know what makes your spouse happy? Have you both ever tried to just be happy in your marriage? If you make serving your spouse a priority and commit to meeting his or her needs, you'll find that the level of happiness in your marriage will increase exponentially.

Remember the childhood song: "If you're happy and you know it, clap your hands. If you're happy and you know it, clap your hands. If you're happy and you know it, then your face will really show it. If you're happy and you know it, clap your hands." The problem within many Christian marriages is that they're very unhappy and it shows. Bitter, negative relationships between married couples are a poor testimony for singles and other couples who might be looking to your example about having a Godly marriage. Clearly, the high divorce rates in and out of the church demonstrate that something has gone wrong in the marital happiness department. The Body of Christ needs to reexamine its priorities to make sure that our witness to others is in alignment with the Word of God. Happiness is based on a choice, not on how good or bad things are going in your life. Don't allow your happiness to change based on how your spouse treats you or on the circumstances of your life. You have the Greater One living in you. Stay in the presence of God because in His presence is fullness of joy. If we're happy and we know it, then our marriages should show it. Say Amen!

Scriptures (KJV)

Psalm 35:9	"And my soul shall be joyful in the LORD: it shall rejoice in his salvation."
Psalm 144:15	"Happy is that people, that is in such a case: yea, happy is that people, whose God is the Lord."

Exercise

Commit a full day to just being happy and to making your spouse's day happy by not complaining, criticizing or expressing any negative comments. Find something that you can do to make your spouse's day happier. At the end of the day, write on the following pages and talk about how the experience made you feel.

Confession

Today, I will find a new way to make my spouse happy.

____

____

____

____

____

____

____

____

____

DAY 14:

FORGIVENESS - THE KEY

Let it go? Are you serious? You don't know what they did to me. Well, without being too blunt, it doesn't matter. We are commanded to love and to forgive. Period. Love covers a multitude of sin; just as while we were yet in sin, God's love covered us. Forgiveness, however, has the ability to remove sin. Forgiveness doesn't necessarily mean that we forget the offense. We all have memories. Forgiveness means choosing not to bring up or relive the offense ever again. Unfortunately we often recall the negative to the exclusion of the positive. It's hard to move forward with the burden of unforgiveness holding us back. The true power of forgiveness is not forgetting; it's the ability to cease the sensation of pain related to what has occurred. True healing takes true forgiveness. The good news is that God is the ultimate healer. When we submit our hurts and our hearts to Him, He will relieve the pain and offense and help us to forgive and move on.

In Matthew 18, there is a parable about a man who owed the king a large sum of money. The king knew he could never pay and forgave the man the debt. Not long afterwards, the man whose debt was forgiven found a man who owed him much less money and demanded he pay or be thrown in debtor's prison.

The man had been forgiven, but he refused to forgive someone who owed him much less. When the ruler found out about it, he threw the man into debtor's prison. Some of us are like this in our marriages, we refuse to forgive, yet we want to be forgiven. We judge our spouse by their actions, but want to be judged by our intentions. Be careful though, because the same measure you use to judge someone else will be used to judge you, too.

In Philippians 3:14, the Apostle Paul told us to press towards the mark for the prize of the high calling in Christ Jesus; forgetting those things behind us. Forgetting is going on and acting as though the offense never occurred. In all of our relationships, we have had episodes of doing things either knowingly or unknowingly that have caused a lot of pain or questions about the person we married, their intent and motive, and their ability to be true to the marriage covenant. Since we have already made the decision and commitment to stay together, "*forgiveness is the key to our future.*" You must be willing to ask for forgiveness and be willing to receive forgiveness, rather than just moving on without settling differences. *Learn to lay aside every weight in this case for the greater goal and purpose, a Marriage Made EZ. (ref.* Hebrews 12:1)

DeeDee has had to forgive me for some things that have seemingly hurt her beyond anything I could have imagined and the same is true for me. We don't pretend as though they never occurred, but we have chosen not to allow any offense to dominate our relationship. Instead, we keep the vision for our marriage at the forefront of everything we say and do. This is a major component of our success. You have the power within you to overcome every hurt that has occurred in your relationship. Employ the spirit of forgiveness and overcome your issues.

We have counseled so many people who have not been able to let go of past hurts and they have become paralyzed, unable to go any further. I know sometimes the pain of the situation clouds our vision and hinders us from being able to see our way through; but if we would look to Jesus—the Author and Finisher of our faith—we would be able to forgive others as He has forgiven us. Although we are spirit beings, it is not my intention to spiritualize everything. Most married people in the body of Christ already know their spiritual responsibilities. They just need practical ways to overcome obstacles in their relationship. My intent is to be as practical as possible without preaching to you and give you biblical principles in a practical way to ensure a promising and positive outcome.

Quite frankly, I don't know if there is anything more beautiful and powerful than one's ability to forgive. When the woman was found in adultery, the people expected Jesus to do what the law demanded in her situation. Jesus, in His infinite wisdom, paused to write in the sand and then said, "He that is without sin, let him cast the first stone." All of us would have had to drop our rocks. We all have sinned in some way. Although your sin may not have happened within the confines of marriage, we all have done something for which we need forgiveness. Sometimes it seems more difficult when others are aware of infidelity in a relationship or even if there is a child that has resulted from that infidelity. I don't mean to sound cold or callous, but gather yourself, "man up" and do what you have to do. Your ability to overcome has a lot to do with your ability to humble yourself. (James 4:10) (We discuss this further on Day 23.) The spirit of pride will try to convince you that it's foolish to remain in a marriage devastated by infidelity. You must know what you want and go after it, regardless of what people think or say. I have divorced myself from the opinions of people. I suggest you do the same.

Your vision, goals and love should be a chief motivator for forgiveness. You must acknowledge the power that exceeds where you are and allow it to motivate you in knowing nothing is worth keeping you from reaching your goal. On Day 10, we discussed vision. Your vision gives you incentive and encourages you to not allow anything to prevent you from getting what God has entitled you to from the foundation of the world. DeeDee will often say, "Look what I would have missed out on if I had quit back when things were tough."

Just as vision and love are chief motivators to forgiveness, rebellion is a chief obstacle to forgiveness. The enemy has robbed you long enough from enjoying your marriage and your life. Don't allow him to rob you of the future that God has ordained for you. The Word of God says that rebellion is as witchcraft. Don't wait until there is absolute hell in your marriage before you seek Jesus. Even if it has reached that point already, remember, when we were at our worst, we were put on friendly terms by the sacrificial death of Jesus. DeeDee and I are having victory because we have chosen to live a resurrected lifestyle. And just like ours, your marriage was intended to be a blessing to more people than just you and your spouse.

Some of us are hindered by the need to forgive ourselves. We often are our own worst critics and enemies. Jesus died for the redemption of our sins. All we have to do is accept the work of Christ on the cross. Revelation 21 says that there is a new heaven and a new earth. John says that Jesus threw our sins into the depths of the sea. Isaiah says that our sins are not remembered anymore. All of this simply means that our sins are not resurrected before the Almighty God. Why do we focus on them? Why are we still bringing them up? Even more so, why do we resurrect the sins of our spouses? Choose to forgive them.

Forgive and relinquish the ability to ever mention the violation again.

Scriptures (KJV)

Matthew 6:14-15	"For if ye forgive men their trespasses, your heavenly Father will also forgive you. But if ye forgive not men their trespasses, neither will your Father forgive your trespasses."
Roman 3:23	"For all have sinned, and come short of the glory of God."
1 John 1:9	"If we confess our sins, he is faithful and just to forgive us our sins, and to cleanse us from all unrighteousness."

Scriptures (MSG)

Matthew 18:21-22	"At that point Peter got up the nerve to ask, 'Master, how many times do I forgive a brother or sister who hurts me? Seven?' Jesus replied, 'Seven! Hardly. Try seventy times seven.'"
Hebrews 12:1	"Wherefore seeing we also are compassed about with so great a cloud of witnesses, let us lay **aside every weight**, and the sin which doth so easily beset us, and let us run with patience the race that is set before us."
James 4:7-10	"So let God work his will in you. Yell a loud no to the Devil and watch him scamper. Say a quiet yes to God and

he'll be there in no time. Quit dabbling in sin. Purify your inner life. Quit playing the field. Hit bottom, and cry your eyes out. The fun and games are over. Get serious, really serious. Get down on your knees before the Master; it's the only way you'll get on your feet."

Exercise

Just love!!! That offense that you've been throwing up in the face of your spouse, cover it and move on. Don't mention it now or ever again. Make a decision, say a prayer and let it go.

Confession

Today I confess my sins to God, knowing that He will forgive me and cleanse me and give me a new start. In the same manner that God has loved and forgiven me, I will love and forgive others who have offended me.

____

____

____

____

____

____

____

____

____

DAY 15:

FRIENDSHIP

One of the smartest moves a single person can make is to marry someone they consider a friend, because by definition they will already have mutual interests and something in common with that individual – with or without romantic attraction and passion.

An ideal marriage is a lifelong friendship between two souls that God has united together as one. Just because you marry your best friend doesn't mean that you don't still have to work on improving and sustaining your marriage. Be a friend to your husband or wife. Be a confidante to them. Be a loving partner. And have fun together!

Have you noticed how serious everyone seems to be lately? Everybody is so busy, so overextended, so distracted and so preoccupied. When do people stop their lives long enough to simply enjoy them? It's ironic how people struggle to have fun with their spouses, but have no problem kicking back and enjoying time with their friends.

When is the last time you and your spouse went on an actual date – no children, no paper placemats, and no distractions other than looking into each other's eyes? It has probably been too long or not often enough. Make a point to schedule a weekly or monthly time that's reserved just for the two of you. Many couples miss the mark when they have children and focus all their time and energy on child rearing, while their marriage slowly deteriorates and dies on the vine. Yes, younger children need our time and attention, but so do our mates. When you made the commitment to love, honor, and cherish one another, those responsibilities did not cease just because your family size increased. As a matter of fact, the best parenting model you can provide for your children is a stable home environment with two loving parents who genuinely love, support and respect each other.

Take time to be a couple, and take time to be a family. Visit parks together, go to the movies, take walks together, have uninterrupted conversations that reinforce your friendship and strengthen your relationship. Discuss your dreams and desires together. Take the time to get to know each other all over again.

Do you remember how your relationship was in the very beginning, when emotions were running high and passion was hot and heavy? Although time and familiarity may have lessened the intensity of those feelings, make it a priority to focus on the things that first brought you together. Discover new hobbies and pastimes that you both enjoy. And don't forget the benefit of fellowship with other Godly couples with whom you can share and enjoy life.

Ask yourself a question: "Is my spouse my friend?" or rather, ask your spouse, "Am I your friend?" If yes, then work on how to deepen that friendship. If no, then you know where to begin. Be intentional about spending more time together and asking probing questions that allow you to know them more intimately. Today's exercise offers some questions to get you started.

Scripture(KJV)

Proverbs 18:24 "A man that hath friends must shew himself friendly: and there is a friend that sticketh closer than a brother."

Exercises

What can you do to make your spouse more comfortable sharing things with you? Come up with guidelines for those conversations. Maybe lean on your friendship to create a safe environment for your spouse to share. Here are some questions and conversation starters you can use:

- Replay for your spouse the moment you knew he/she was the one.
- What is your favorite color? Is there a reason why?
- What do you think makes your spouse smile? Were you right?
- What is your favorite marriage memory?
- What is your favorite relationship moment?
- When you think of intimacy, what do you think of?
- What does your spouse do to make you feel loved and nurtured?
- What has your spouse taught you?
- Are we having fun with each other?

Record the answers on the following pages.

Confession

I am a good friend to my spouse and maintain an environment where he/she is comfortable sharing anything with me. (Say it. Tell them.)

MarriageMade

INTERLUDE

Here we are roughly at the half-way point in this book. You may be saying, "This is tough." I warned you that a *Marriage Made EZ* would be. Don't be discouraged. It's just as DeeDee often says, "Believers often become discouraged because they have been taught the promises of God, without being taught the process. With every promise, plan, or prophecy, there is a process for bringing it into fruition – instructions that need to be followed." The processes are built on faith. We must take hold of our measure of faith to help bring about everything that you believe you can. The steps in the process are: (1) accepting Christ, (2) believing Christ above everything else, (3) believing in those things which aren't, (4) studying the Word so that you can speak the promises into existence, (5) speaking life into your personal valley of dry bones, as Ezekiel did, and (6) heeding the instructions, without fail, as given by your man or woman of God.

Know that working the Word for your marriage requires faith and endurance. You may not see instant results. You can be sure though that the seeds you sow to restore your marriage will produce a greater harvest. Galatians 6:7 says, "Do not be deceived, God is not mocked, for whatever a man sows, that he will also reap." Great marriages don't just develop – they are built. Your work of faith and labor of love will not be in vain.

Take dominion over your relationship, and you will not only have created a new vision for your marriage, you will have created a foundation for a marriage that is built to last. For the remainder of this book, continue drilling into those dry areas of your marriage to release the gift, the anointing and the contribution that God has called for you to bring forth this year. Your marriage is worth it. Here's my prayer and declaration over you, your spouse and your marriage:

> ***Father, thank you for helping my brother and sister in Christ persevere and make their marriage a priority. I pray that you give them the strength and courage they need to endure and to see this process through until they achieve victory. In Jesus' name... I stand with this couple and declare that every good thing there is in my and DeeDee's lives be added to theirs. I declare by the word of God that you prosper in all that you set your hands to do and that no natural or spiritual weapon formed against you shall prosper nor shall any plague come near your dwelling. I declare that you reign in life as the head and not the tail. In Jesus name . . . AMEN***

You will make it if you don't give up. Let's keep moving.

DAY 16:

DON'T QUIT: STAY IN IT TO WIN IT

As I begin this session, let me just make it crystal clear that there is nothing in this entire book that is to be used as a reason or excuse to leave your marriage. God hates divorce, and the only reason that there was an allowance made was because of the condition of the heart of man. Matthew 19:7-8 reads, "They say unto him, Why did Moses then command to give a writing of divorcement, and to put her away? He saith unto them, Moses because of the hardness of your hearts suffered you to put away your wives: but from the beginning it was not so." We were given divorce as an option because we have not mastered the art of forgiveness. Assuming that you have read all of the previous chapters of this book and applied the lessons therein, I choose to believe that you really want your marriage and can see it thriving beyond your wildest expectations.

In the off chance that you have come to this chapter and are no further along, I want to take this opportunity to be very clear. You must work to have a thriving marriage. You must decide that surviving is simply not enough. That being said, there are some extenuating circumstances for which divorce is allowed. I call them the 3As: adultery, abuse, and addiction.

By Webster's definition, adultery is the voluntary sexual intercourse between a married person and someone other than his or her lawful spouse. As Christians, our definition of adultery is even broader as it includes not just physical sex, but the emotional attachment that lays the groundwork for adultery. Emotional connections with people of the opposite sex can be created through sharing the intimate details of your marriage, especially your problems. This creates a false intimacy which causes a false connection and lays the groundwork for you to be unfaithful to your spouse. At all costs, avoid having conversations about your marriage with people that you don't have a counseling relationship with. Very often, the other person is someone of the opposite sex at work, of social media or wherever it is that you spend the majority of your time. Learn to recognize the trap of the enemy so that you can avoid this occurrence.

Even where adultery has been committed, it doesn't mean that you have to divorce your spouse. Oneness can be restored if both parties are willing to do the work of restoration. Divorce is not to be considered lightly. The repercussions of divorce are great - not just for the couple, but upon their children and their families and friends. Consider thoughtfully and seek Godly counsel before pursuing divorce as a course of action.

Webster's dictionary defines abuse as to use wrongly or improperly; misuse; to treat in a harmful, injurious, or offensive way; to speak insultingly, harshly, and unjustly to or about; revile; malign. Notice that the definition of abuse is very broad even though it can be broken into two different categories: physical and mental. Of course, if someone is putting their hands on you in a threatening, harmful, "abusive" way, you must get out. Your life is in danger. There are stories on the news everyday of men and women who have been hurt by their abusive spouses. Yes, you need to pray for them, but pray for them from across town.

Much less noticeable, somehow more tolerable, but definitely as destructive, is the torment of mental/verbal abuse. The Bible says that death and life are in the power of the tongue. If you're not speaking words of encouragement that lift up your spouse, it is possible that you are being abusive. It is even possible to be abusive in your attitude towards your spouse. If that is the case, you must stop it immediately. Seek the help of a counselor. Get help immediately, especially if your family means anything at all to you.

Webster's defines addiction as the state of being enslaved to a habit or practice or to something that is psychologically or physically habit-forming, as narcotics, to such an extent that its cessation causes severe trauma. When an individual gets hooked on a substance, the whole family suffers the consequences. By nature, addictions do not improve over time without intervention. What might start out as a physical addiction eventually will morph into an emotional and physiological addiction that literally changes the physical, mental and emotional makeup of the person. The Bible tells us that to whomever or whatever we yield our members, that becomes our master. If your spouse refuses to submit to God, but instead yields his or her body and mind to some addictive substance, get help or get out; protect yourself and your family.

In all of these cases, you can choose to quit on your marriage. You can also choose NOT to quit. Quitting is the easy part, but it takes a fully-surrendered Christian, one that is sold-out and walking in faith to hang in there through thick and thin. I believe that's you!

Quitting on your marriage doesn't just mean divorce. Quitting means looking for love in all the wrong places. Quitting means running back to mom and dad complaining about what your spouse isn't doing right. Quitting is giving your spouse the silent treatment and emotionally withdrawing instead of communicating and working through your problems. Quitting is sitting back and doing nothing while your marriage deteriorates due to neglect.

Please don't quit. Don't let the devil win. Don't let the world's broken system convince you that your marriage is beyond repair. The God we serve is the way, the truth, and the life. That means you have God's authority to speak life back into your marriage. You serve the most High God who has the power of resurrection in His hand. You can put your lifeless, loveless marriage into the Creator's hands and ask Him to breathe new life into it and into you and your spouse. He has put His life, authority and ability in our hands. We must make it happen and He has our back.

A Word of Encouragement Just for You...

Be encouraged that you are not alone in the struggle and fight to save your marriage. As a matter of fact, most likely you are in the majority because marriage and families are under spiritual attack. However, here is some good news for couples. GOD IS ON YOUR SIDE! God is rooting for your marriage. God can and will answer your prayers, because restoring your marriage is His will. Keeping your family intact is His will. Demonstrating the love of Christ in the marriage relationship is His desire for your life. You are more than conquerors through Christ Jesus and God will give you the strength and the courage you need to win the battle against divorce, dishonor, deception and disappointment. Yes, there are trials and tribulations that you will have to face and sometimes unexpected circumstances will catch you off guard. But rest assured in knowing that the battle is not yours, it's the Lord's!

Scriptures (KJV)

2 Corinthians 2:14	"Now thanks be unto God, which always causeth us to triumph in Christ, and maketh manifest the savour of his knowledge by us in every place."
2 Corinthians 12:9	"My grace is sufficient for thee: for my strength is made perfect in weakness. Most gladly therefore will I rather glory in my infirmities, that the power of Christ may rest upon me."

Scriptures (MSG)

1 John 4:4-6	"My dear children, you come from God and belong to God. You have already won a big victory over those false teachers, for the Spirit in you is far stronger than anything in the world. These people belong to the Christ-denying world. They talk the world's language and the world eats it up. But we come from God and belong to God. Anyone who knows God understands us and listens. The person who has nothing to do with God will, of course, not listen to us. This is another test for telling the Spirit of Truth from the spirit of deception."

Exercise

Look your spouse in the eye and tell him/her what he/she means to you. What were his/her attributes that made you want to marry him/her in the first place? Tell your spouse what he/she means to you. Reaffirm your commitment never to leave one another and repeat these words: "I love you. And I will honor my vow to this covenant relationship." Continue holding hands and pray together, asking God to give you wisdom to rebuild your marriage and to restore the life in your marriage.

Confession

I am fearfully and wonderfully made in the image of God and will only seek to do those things that glorify Him. I will not quit or give up on my marriage.

____

____

____

____

____

____

____

____

____

____

____

DAY 17: MAINTAINING A SPIRIT OF FAITH - FAITH IT TIL YOU MAKE IT

There's a big difference between faking it and "faithing" it. Faking it is acting like it and not wanting it in your heart. Faithing it is acting like it and wanting it in your heart. You can't fake your way to a good marriage. You have to faith your way to it. You have to want it, and you have to be willing to work for it.

We are commanded to live by faith 24/7/365. (Twenty-four hours a day, seven days a week, 365 days a year.) All the promises of God are accessed by faith. Some think they are operating in faith and really aren't. There is a partnership in this faith covenant that we have with God. This means that we have a role to play in our success. Some people expect God to do His part and to do our part as well. They say things like, "If I take one step, God will take two." How unscriptural is that! The Bible says in Mark 9:23, "Jesus said unto him, If thou canst believe, **all things** are **possible** to him that believeth." That Scripture shows us clearly the partnership agreement we have with our Lord. The phrase that says, "All things are possible" is God's part. The phrase that says "To them that believe" is our part. We must have an unfeigned confidence that says that if this thing doesn't work out, then the world will stop rotating.

There are four functioning components of faith: Believing, Receiving, Speaking and Acting. Whatever you believe you will receive, will cause you to speak and act accordingly. What we believe is largely resultant of our hearing. We must study to show ourselves approved, especially since faith only comes by hearing, not by trials or tribulations.

If Abraham is an example of a man of faith, and he is, we need to study what he did and duplicate his actions in our lives. Since God is no respecter of persons, what He did for Abraham, He will do for us as well. We know that Abraham called those things which weren't as though they were. He believed according to what was spoken to Him by God. He chose to be occupied with the promise and not the problems, and He gave praise to God in advance. We must use this same model for our marriages. We must do the following:

(1) believe we have a *Marriage Made EZ,*

(2) receive, by faith, our *Marriage Made EZ*;

(3) speak that we have a *Marriage Made EZ,* and

(4) act as if we have our *Marriage Made EZ.*

We must be moved only by what we believe, not by what we feel or see.

There's a video I saw of a pit bull. In the video, the pit bull locked its jaws around a stick held by its handler. The handler was able to pick that pit bull up and swing him around on the stick! That's the kind of faith that we must have for our marriages, the kind that will not allow us to let go, no matter what. Never let what you feel dominate your will. That's worth repeating. NEVER LET WHAT YOU FEEL DOMINATE YOUR

WILL. Hold fast to your profession of faith and *F*ind *A*nswers *I*n *T*he *H*eart! Say it with me, *F*orsaking *A*ll *I* *T*rust *H*im!

Scriptures (KJV)

Galatians 3:11	"But that no man is justified by the law in the sight of God, it is evident: for, the just shall live by faith."
James 2:26	"For as the body without the spirit is dead, so faith without works is dead also."
Hebrews 11:6	"But without faith it is impossible to please him: for he that cometh to God must believe that he is, and that he is a rewarder of them that diligently seek him."

Exercises

On the following pages, write a faith confession for the marriage you want to have. Use the four steps above to formulate it.

Confession

Use the confession that you wrote in the exercise above.

____

____

____

____

____

____

____

DAY 18:

OUR INNER CIRCLE - INLAWS AND OUTLAWS

The Word of God says that you will become known by the company you keep. Associations are everything. If you hang around 9 broke people, you're bound to be the 10th. If you hang around 9 wealthy people, you're bound to be the 10th. So, be careful who and what influences you allow in your life and around your marriage. Ask yourself these questions: who am I around; what are they doing to me and my marriage and do I like it? If your associations are not keeping you in the mindset of building your marriage, you need some new associations.

One of the more difficult transitions for newlyweds is "forsaking all others" and leaving behind single friends and the routines of single life. Once you're married, your first commitment is to your spouse; and you must set boundaries that are in alignment with that commitment around every other relationship in your life. Husbands, even though you may have spent every Friday night of the last 10 years hanging out on boys' night with your single buddies, those days are over. Wives, yes it's true that your single girlfriends are a lot of fun, but let's be clear that their priorities are different from yours now and your husband and household must come first. This is not to say that your friends are bad people. The point is that when your status in life changes, your associations must change as well. Sometimes, honoring your spouse will mean discontinuing those relationships which make him/her uncomfortable. If your spouse is your help meet, and he/she is (Genesis 2:18), then you must believe that he/she will, at times, have insights into the motives of the opposite sex that you won't have. The question becomes, who am I yielding greater influence than the voice of my God-chosen spouse?

Even the conversations that you used to have as a single person will be different once you are married. 1 Corinthians 15:33 states, "Be not deceived: evil communications corrupt good manners." What you talk about will undoubtedly influence how you treat and communicate with your spouse. If you're still hanging out with single friends who inevitably talk about how to meet members of the opposite sex, those thoughts are going to start taking root in your mind.

Husbands, you know your single buddies better than anyone. Do you really want them spending too much time around you and your wife? They may not be bad people, but even good people with good intentions can quickly end up in bad situations.

It's often said that you can find out everything you need to know about someone by the five people closest to them. Where we spend our time and who we spend it with is a direct reflection of who we really are. Take a look at your inner circle. Who are the primary influencers in your life? Are you surrounded with Godly, mature couples who can share their life lessons with you and mentor your marriage? Or are you around spiritually immature individuals who have a negative toll on your marriage? There are people that we allow to reside in the inner circle or front row of the stadium of our life. Then there are others, who should be on the 5th or 6th row. Still, there are others who should be in the parking lot. Allow your spouse to help you to determine who is who, since his/her perspective is often one that we don't have.

My sister Gloria was a great example of entertaining negative associations. Around our house, Bishop (my father) had a rule. That rule was that when the streetlights came on, we had better be in the house. My sisters Gloria and DD and my brother Dewayne and I were out playing, when the lights came on. Everyone except Gloria ran home immediately. Gloria, listening to her friends, even verbalized that she wasn't coming home with us. Of course, when we got home, Bishop asked where she was and I was the one to tell him that Gloria said, "she wasn't coming home." Bishop went to the tree, broke off a switch, slid the leaves off, went and found Gloria, and beat her all the way home. (For those who don't know what a switch is and weren't able to ascertain it from the sentence, it's a small branch from a tree used for disciplining children.) Now Gloria, rather than running, like most sensible kids would have done, walked home, while getting beat, all because she was listening to the voice of her friends. I couldn't believe she didn't know that it was time to run! Obviously, Gloria was listening to poor counsel, people who should have been in the parking lot of her life, and she paid the price for it. (She's going to get me for sharing this story!)

We must be very careful about whose counsel we accept and whose advice we follow. Everyone around you isn't always good for you. We often tell our newlyweds to spend the majority of their time listening to people who have been successful in marriage. Although it is possible that you can learn from those who have not been successful, some are overly jaded by the negativity that they have experienced. A lot of times, these well-meaning people can serve to create doubt in your mind about the decision that you've already made – to grow your marriage relationship with your current spouse. Truly, all the enemy want is to bring doubt to your marriage, since doubt is an enemy to our faith. Doubt is the doorway to every distraction, and it offers alternatives that we've already denounced. We must get rid of the *IF*s once and for all. Speak boldly. Speak loudly what you are believing God to do. That's the only way to dispel doubt.

When you married your wife or husband, you probably didn't anticipate all the things that would come along with having in-laws. Sometimes they are meddlesome or rude; sometimes they lead lifestyles that aren't conducive to the path you want to follow for your household. But... you cannot simply abandon them because after all, they're family now.

Dealing with in-laws can be tricky. But the good news is that there isn't an overbearing father-in-law or a condescending mother-in-law that prayer, fasting, discussion, and moving further away can't fix. Getting to know your in-laws can provide incredible insight into why your spouse does the things he/she does. In-laws can provide an in-depth perspective into your spouse's background, upbringing, values, and perspective. You can also learn about habits, beliefs, and generational influences that might otherwise take years or decades to discover. Being able to witness—up close and personal—how and why your mate does the things he/she does based on how he/she grew up can be extremely helpful in understanding your spouse and working on your marriage. In-laws give you a front-row seat for understanding why your spouse is the way he or she is. Observing the relationship between parent and child also provides an opportunity to anticipate how your spouse might react to a future situation or problem – based on his/her upbringing. So don't despise the relationships; capitalize and learn from them. Use the information to your advantage.

There are two very dangerous situations we see in counseling sessions: first is the propensity to talk with your parents, cousins, friends, anyone outside of your relationship, about the things that are going wrong in your marriage. "He did this" and "she did that." This is very dangerous in that everyone in your life is not in favor of your marriage or your being happy. As sad as it is to have to say this, it's absolutely true. With that in mind, they may give you bad advice, even encouraging you to leave, so they can have a chance with your spouse! What you really need is encouragement to grow through the current challenges, so that you can ultimately enjoy long-term success in your marriage. Additionally, once you and your spouse get past the rough spot and you've forgiven one another, your family members aren't so gracious. They won't forget. When you pour a vial of poison into a pond, it's nearly impossible to get the poison out, so that the pond becomes viable to sustain life once again. It's the same thing with your family and friends. Once you've told them how awful your spouse is, it's very difficult for them to forget what you told them and act as if nothing ever happened. Don't dishonor your spouse by talking about him or her negatively, even in anger, to anyone. To dishonor your spouse is to dishonor yourself. After all, you and your spouse are one.

The second dangerous situation we see is the improper order of relational priorities, which we discuss on Day 25. The biblical command regarding marriage is for the son or daughter to "leave" the parental home and "cleave" as one to the spouse. That means mom is no longer the first woman in his life; and dad is no longer the first-priority man in her life. Believe it or not, your spouse takes precedent over your parents (and your children). Once you've made a choice and entered into a covenant with God and your spouse, that covenant becomes the primary relationship in your life. It doesn't mean that you value or love your parents less; it simply means that your life has a new set of priorities that place husbands and wives at the top of the list. Remember Day 2, "Leave, Cleave, and Weave."

That being said, the Bible does command us to honor our parents. Because you are married, his parents become your parents and her parents become your parents. To have long life and to have things go well for you, you must honor them. I didn't say you have to like them. I said honor them. (Even though I can't imagine why you would marry a person whose parents you didn't like since most people grow up to be substantially similar to their parents.)

It's often said that you don't just marry your spouse, you marry the entire family. That's not true, if both spouses are willing to establish and build a marriage the way God intended, meaning a mutual, joint agreement that "what God has put together, let no man (or mother-in-law) put asunder." If, indeed, a marriage encounters conflict due to spousal and in-law conflict, there must first be a meeting of the minds based on the Word of God. How would God have us respond to this situation? What would Jesus want us to do in order to respect our marriage vows, but also to honor our parents? Somewhere in the middle is common ground. It doesn't mean it's easy or convenient, but *Marriage Made EZ* must follow God's order.

Fortunately, DeeDee and I have Godly parents who are more interested in seeing God's Will accomplished in our lives than they are in meddling. Although her parents were not in favor of her marrying me, now, having gone through the process, we all live together, in the same house, without the delineation of "my parents" and "her parents.' Our individual parents have become our collective parents. What an incredible gift to give your spouse and your children. If you have outlaws, you and your spouse must create a viable strategy to keep them in line and out of your marriage.

Scriptures (KJV)

Genesis 2:24	"Therefore shall a man leave his father and his mother, and shall cleave unto his wife: and they shall be one flesh."
Proverbs 12:5	"The thoughts of the righteous are right: but the counsels of the wicked are deceit."
Proverbs 13:20	"He that walketh with wise men shall be wise: but a companion of fools shall be destroyed."

Exercise

Use your new found communications skills to discuss with your spouse any relationships that make you uneasy. Discuss the parameters of those relationships to make sure they do not have a negative influence on your marriage. Also, discuss whether or not those parameters mean severing the relationship with the offending individual(s).

Write down a recent example of when you allowed an outside influence to interfere with your marital relationship. Discuss how things could have been handled differently, and then agree with your spouse that he or she has first priority in your life.

Confession

Say this prayer, "I am known by the company I keep. Thank you, Father, for exposing, revealing, and removing from my life everyone and everything that does not have my best interest at heart."

DAY 19:

MASTER YOUR MONEY, RATHER THAN MONEYMASTERING YOU

In a perfect world, money would not be an issue. Unfortunately, we don't live in a perfect world. If we did, Christians would pay their tithes, put money in savings, invest wisely and have an abundance to meet their needs. However, for many—dare I say most— that simply is not the case. Money is an issue and it's a very big one. We've all heard it said, "Money is evil." What a horrible mischaracterization of the Word of God. The actual Scripture says that the love of money is the root of all evil . . . not money itself. (1 Tim. 6:10) In actuality, the *lack* of money is evil. Think of all the things you have needed to do, even for God, that you haven't been able to do because of a lack of money. Exactly. Pure evil.

Money is neutral - neither bad nor good. Money takes on the character of the person who has it. Whether you have a little or a lot, the secret to avoiding monetary blow-ups is open communication. From the very start, to the very end, it is imperative that both spouses honestly and clearly express their understanding and expectations about household financial goals and habits. Couples need to create a budget and then stick to it.

It's fine to have a separate personal "unrestricted" account for family fun or vacations, but it is necessary to have a joint household account that has clear parameters set to cover the family's financial obligations. Even if you're "not good with numbers or budgeting," don't use that as an excuse to be uninvolved. It's important to talk about money together as a couple and to find mutually beneficial and agreeable ways to finance your future together.

The topic of money is often the source of power struggles within a marriage. For example, because *he* makes all of the money, *she* shouldn't have any say over how it's spent. Or because *she* is the primary breadwinner, *his* opinion isn't valid or doesn't carry as much weight in important financial decisions. That's dangerous. Couples need to remember that they're on the same side – regardless of who makes what. When you got married, you gave up "mine" for "ours" and "what's yours is hers and what's hers is hers" in favor of "what's ours is ours."

In the beginning of our marriage, DeeDee made the majority of the money in our household. This was never a place for contention because she didn't "lord it over me." This means that although we both knew that she made the most money, she didn't use it to emasculate me or minimize my contributions to the family finances. She protected me and never used language or even made decisions that spoke "This is my money." So when your wife makes most of the money, quit trippin' – the money is in your house!

However, this wasn't always my revelation. There was a time that DeeDee and I took a trip to the Bahamas. I remember having some negative feelings about the trip because it was her money that paid for it. When we arrived in the Bahamas, I had an epiphany. When the bellhop picked up our luggage to take it to our room, he had no idea who had paid for the trip. So I dropped it, the entire thought and feeling, right there in the Bahamas and haven't picked it up since. I suggest you do the same. Think about it, Adam lost everything in one day and still, he and Eve walked out of the garden together . . . broke. Now look at what they've built. Let's not allow money to be the cause for the break-up of our homes and marriages.

One of the most important questions you will answer in your marriage is 'Who handles the money?" Does that also mean that they control the decisions to spend it? The money in our house is handled by DeeDee. She receives the income, handles the banking and pays the bills. When there are issues or questions, we discuss them. On a regular basis, she gives me a report of our financial affairs to make sure I have a complete understanding of our position. Even though I don't handle the day-to-day money management responsibilities, I'm still aware of where our money is, so that we are in agreement about important financial matters.

DeeDee also points out that we had to be aware of the difference between a need and a want. If there was a need, then we talked to God about it before making any decisions or signing any contracts. We recognize that just as there are seasons in the natural, there are seasons in the spiritual, moments of optimal timing for making certain financial decisions. For instance, while a growing family may absolutely need a house or a larger apartment, moving forward at a time where layoffs are raging in a place of employment may not be wise. Another example is while a vehicle may be a need, a luxury vehicle when you are not a homeowner may not be a wise purchase.

Your ability to master your finances is going to be directly related to your ability to create a viable financial plan. Every financial plan should at least have these components:

1. Tithing. When you become committed to and consistent in paying tithes and giving offerings, you put yourself in a position to receive from God.

2. Savings/Investment. An effective savings plan should be developed with defined goals in mind. Whether you are saving for a new home, your child's college tuition, or retirement, separate accounts should be part of the plan.

3. Obliterate debt. The Bible says that we should owe no man anything but love. We must get a clear understanding of credit and debt and be aware of what it really costs us each time we use our credit cards. Suffice it to say that if you can't pay for it in cash, you shouldn't be putting it on a credit card either.

4. Provision for Generational Wealth. The Bible says that a wise man leaves an inheritance for his children and his children's children. We must be more interested in setting up a financial plan for our children than we are about materialistic things.

Part of providing for your family includes making sure that your last will and testament, your living will, trusts and other estate planning documents are in order. This is a simple way to avoid family fighting and dysfunction with just a little planning. You must have a will. In many states, your prior spouse would be entitled to your current assets, even if you've remarried, if you die without a will. Don't put your spouse in a position to have to fight after you leave. Protect them in death, just as you would in life.

Remember, money can trigger very strong emotions. When the money isn't right in a household, often nothing else is right either. Frustrations over money can affect communication, attitudes, and intimacy. If a man doesn't feel like he is adequately able to provide for his family, those negative emotions are going to show through. If she doesn't feel secure in her own home or feel like her needs are met, then those negative emotions are going to raise their ugly heads and impact the relationship. Don't allow it. It's vital to make sure the money situation is right to keep intimacy intact. The need for security is crucial for most women. A viable financial plan, complete with open and honest communication, goes a long way to adding security to her life.

All of that being said, like many Americans, you may be in a position where money is a major issue in your household. At the time that this book is being written, there are an abundance of economic issues abounding. There are a record number of foreclosures and unemployment is at an all-time high. It's also essential to stay in faith as it concerns money. We decided that we would not participate in the economic downturn. Recession is a foreign word to our family, and it can be for yours as well. The absolute worse response to financial challenges is to ignore them as if they don't exist. Get counsel and get a book on finances; you must pass this test to have a testimony. That's all financial challenges are ... a test; this too shall pass. The bottom line for marital and financial peace is to make sure that you master your money and that your money doesn't master you.

Scriptures (MSG)

Matthew 6:24	"You can't worship two gods at once. Loving one god, you'll end up hating the other. Adoration of one feeds contempt for the other. You can't worship God and money both."
Luke 14:28	"Is there anyone here who, planning to build a new house, doesn't first sit down and figure the cost so you'll know if you can complete it? If you only get the foundation laid and then run out of money, you're going to look pretty foolish. Everyone passing by will poke fun at you: 'He started something he couldn't finish.'"
James 1:5-8	"If you don't know what you're doing, pray to the Father. He loves to help. You'll get his help and won't be condescended to when you ask for it. Ask boldly, believingly, without a second thought. People who "worry their prayers" are like wind-whipped waves. Don't think you're going to get anything from the Master that way, adrift at sea, keeping all your options open."

Exercise

Have an uninterrupted discussion about money that includes what your goals, desires, and financial expectations are for the next 6, 12, and 24 months. Make sure you have a written plan, including your financial priorities, that you and your spouse refer to on a regular basis. Eliminate any expenditures that take away from the household budget and are not in alignment with your written plan; things that are taking away from the household budget that really can wait.

Which one of you should handle the money? Write down who and why. Share with one another.

Confession

Money will not be my master, rather I will master money. Thank you, Father, that all our needs are met according to your riches in glory, by Christ Jesus, and there's plenty more to put in store.

____

____

____

____

____

____

____

____

____

____

____

____

____

____

DAY 20:

SEX

On the sixth day, God created sex, and it was good. I'm not exactly sure why people get so uncomfortable and bent out of shape when it comes to talking about sex. I mean, think about it... sex is how we all got here in the first place. Whether your parents hooked up in their marriage bed or in the back seat of their '72 Ford Pinto, your existence is due to their having sex. So, even if nobody's talking about it, a lot of people are doing it.

Not only is sex between a husband and wife good... it is good for you. Sex is a great recreational workout, and it also is a great stress reliever. No amount of jogging on a treadmill or pumping iron can compete with the physical and emotional release of tensions and biological endorphins (feel-good hormones) that are produced.

Sex, the way God designed it, is a beautiful and wonderful thing. It is the devil and this fallen world that have distorted sex and made it into something perverse and degrading. In many of my counseling sessions, I see a lot of tension between husbands and wives about sex and intimacy: they are not one in the same. Sex is physical. Intimacy is emotional and physical and creates a bond between the husband and wife to which no one else is privy. Sexual intimacy is a couple's primary way to continually consummate their marital covenant and renew their oneness on every level.

Sexual intimacy is a crucial element of *Marriage Made EZ*. The very biology of sex reinforces oneness when a husband is joined with his wife in sexual intimacy. The union and physical connection of sex actually strengthens the relationship and the bond between husband and wife. In fact, medically speaking, it has been proven that the more sex you have, the longer your life will be. An unsatisfactory or incomplete sex life will absolutely wreak havoc in your marriage.

The deterioration of a healthy, active, and mutually beneficial sex life is the beginning of the end of a good marriage. Why? Sex creates intimacy and brings a couple closer. Sex reunites the couple toward a common cause and focus. The actual exchange during intimacy further unites them and secures their mutual interests toward stability in the relationship. Scripture instructs us as married couples to not "defraud" each other – unless by mutual agreement to fast and pray. In other words, it is dangerous to use or withhold sex as a way to control or manipulate your spouse in a relationship. As a matter of fact, it is unGodly.

When we take marriage vows before God and witnesses, we vow to love, honor and cherish – and we commit our bodies and sexual fidelity to our spouse.

Some of the greatest challenges we see facing couples today include emotional baggage from previous relationships that had a sexual component. When you sleep with someone who is not your husband or wife, you create an eternal bond with them on both a natural and spiritual level. Just because you break up with them doesn't mean those emotional ties are gone. There are a number of abuses and diseases occurring because mankind has chosen to disobey God when it comes to sexual purity and moral responsibility, not to mention the number of children born out of marriage.

Another problem for young married couples is sharing too many private and intimate details about their sex life with friends or family. The marriage bed should be honored and protected. Only if there is a situation where one of the spouses is in danger or being threatened, should intimate details be divulged, and then only to your pastor, ministry leader, or other professionals. A wise person only shares his/her problems with someone in a position to offer a solution. Otherwise, discretion is the better part of valor – and will help fortify the relationship.

Finally, we get a lot of questions about what type of sex is honorable and if anything is off-limits. My response is always that marriage and everything that happens within the marriage should glorify the beauty of intimacy that God designed and should not make either spouse feel dishonored or disrespected. That's where communication comes in. If you are considering different sexual positions or a change in frequency of sex, make sure you talk openly and honestly with your spouse, so that there is no hidden agenda and there are no hurt feelings.

<u>Scriptures (KJV/MSG)</u>

Hebrews 13:4	"Marriage is honorable in all, and the bed undefiled: but whoremongers and adulterers God will judge."
Proverbs 31:10-12	"A good woman is hard to find, and worth far more than diamonds. Her husband trusts her without reserve, and never has reason to regret it. Never spiteful, she treats him generously all her life long."

Exercise

Take the 7 Day Sex Challenge. Have sex with your spouse at least once a day for 7 days in a row. If you miss a day, you must start over!

Together read Song of Solomon 7:6-13 from the Message Bible. Husbands read the man's part and wives read the woman's part.

Confession

I thank God that our desires are to one another and our sex lives are fun and enjoyable.

My body is a temple; it belongs to God and to my spouse; and I take every reasonable effort to remain healthy, active, and attractive.

____

____

____

____

____

____

____

____

____

____

____

DAY 21:

SEX - HER NEEDS

If you didn't already know, men and women are different – especially when it comes to sex. Men, you may not believe or understand this, but there are a lot of women who can and would like to live without sex in their lives. Women, you probably already know this, but the majority of men cannot imagine a life without sex in it.

And therein lies a major part of the problem. The sexual needs of men and women are different. Of course, I'm speaking in general terms, because certainly there are plenty of women with a healthy sexual appetite, and some men who couldn't care less about sex. But those are the exceptions – not the norm.

When God created woman, He created her to be a receptacle of love, a nurturing carrier of life. Sex is inherently more than a physical act for women, because for most of a woman's life, sex has the potential of resulting in the creation of life, an emotional attachment and process that is a permanent part of her forever. Because women equate sex with emotions, they tend to be much more inclined to want love and intimacy before having sex. Intimacy is the toll to move across the bridge to sex. Your goal, husband, is to win her heart.

When God created man, He created him to conquer. Sex is inherently a physical act and source of relief for men. This is even demonstrated in the process of sexual arousal which is usually much faster and shorter for a man than a woman. Men in general tend to be linear in their thought processes and very goal-oriented. That translates to finding a woman for sex, with the goal of sexual fulfillment and maybe procreation.

The bottom line for a happier and more fulfilling marriage is that women need love, intimacy and affection. You've probably heard men and women referred to as a microwave versus a crockpot in the bedroom. For the most part, that analogy is true. You can literally "push a man's button" and instantly he's cooking in the bedroom. A woman needs to simmer all day, warm up gradually and build to a crescendo. By that time, the husband has fallen asleep, leaving his wife to suffer silently and unfulfilled.

If you desire to be a better lover, then start with the biggest sex organ within the human body, the brain. Husbands, ask your wife what turns her on. Ask where and how she likes to be touched. And if she's uncomfortable talking about it at first, ask her to guide your hands—and your heart—and simply show you what she likes. Ask her to describe her ideal sexual encounter. Don't be surprised if it starts with a hidden note or romantic card from you; then a brief phone call just to say hi; maybe a surprise delivery of flowers during the day; reservations for dinner that night; and confirmation that all the household duties or chores have been completed, so that she can focus solely on making love. For most women, sex is as much mental and emotional as it is physical. Lastly, something a lot of men don't grow up learning how to do is be affectionate and actually say the words, "I love you." Men, master the art of saying, "I love you" and show that love, and your entire household will thrive.

Scripture (MSG)

Proverbs 5:17-20

> "Your spring water is for you and you only, not to be passed around among strangers. Bless your fresh-flowing fountain! Enjoy the wife you married as a young man! Lovely as an angel, beautiful as a rose— don't ever quit taking delight in her body. Never take her love for granted! Why would you trade enduring intimacies for cheap thrills with a whore? For dalliance with a promiscuous stranger?"

Exercise

Several times today, call your wife just to tell her you love her. Choose something you know makes her happy and do it for her today.

Confession

I am affectionate and in love with my wife. (You should know what to do next.)

____

____

____

____

____

____

____

DAY 22:

SEX - HIS NEEDS

Here is one of the worst kept secrets in the world... men like sex.

Men want sex.

Men need sex to feel respected, appreciated, and loved.

Wives, here are 5 techniques that you can employ that may further excite your husband. Most of the time, you'll be amazed at how he responds when these things are in place.

1. Initiate sex every now and then. Your husband will not mind at all.

2. Tell your husband that you're attracted to him and why. Men tend to be self-conscious about their bodies (just like many women).

3. Show and tell your husband (gently) how to please you and he will happily oblige. Men are not automatically born to be confident and good lovers.

4. Don't be overly critical and self-conscious about your body. He doesn't want a supermodel (unless you are

one). Your husband likes your body and wants to enjoy it just the way it is.

5. Ask your husband what he enjoys and what turns him on – and then become a willing participant. Not all men enjoy the same things sexually.

Sex was created by God to be a beautiful, wonderful experience between a husband and wife. If either spouse is unwilling to have sex – or finds it uncomfortable or unenjoyable – open, honest communication is crucial to get to the root of the challenge. Certainly, there needs to be prayer, understanding, and mutual support.

Husbands are to love their wives the way Christ loved the church, so there should never be an instance where he is forcing or coercing his wife to do something she is unwilling to do. That is definitely not Christ-like. One of the foundations of a good marriage is agreement, so make sure you both agree in the bedroom, too.

Scripture (MSG)

Ephesians 5:22	"Wives, understand and support your husbands in ways that show your support for Christ. The husband provides leadership to his wife the way Christ does to his church, not by domineering, but by cherishing. So just as the church submits to Christ as he exercises such leadership, wives should likewise submit to their husbands."

Exercise

Wives, take time to get comfortable with your husband's body by touching, teasing and learning what turns him on. If your husband is in agreement with #1 above, tonight, you set the tone, atmosphere and environment for love making. Every marriage is different; for you it could mean candles while for someone else, it could mean the Wonder Woman or French Maid costume.

Confession

I love my husband and have no issues with showing him physically. I treat him generously all my life long.

DAY 23:

HUMILITY AND SUBMISSION - IT'S NOT ABOUT YOU!

In our garage, there are many different vehicles. All of them, of course, have different keys. I can't get into the Bentley using the Mini-Cooper key; I have to use the Mini-Cooper's key to get into the Mini-Cooper. In our offices, however, there are several different keys designated to unlock different doors. One employee can't use his key to access another employee's office. I, on the other hand, have the master key and this master key grants me access into every office. Humility is like the master key that grants you unlimited access to everything you desire. God gives more grace to the humble.

One of the most critical attributes I find missing in relationships is humility. It amazes me how most people feel the need to have their own way in marriage. They say things like "It's my way or the highway" which is completely contrary to the Word of God. We are to submit "our way" unto our *own* spouse (not someone else's). There came a time when I no longer cared about having my way. I knelt down before DeeDee and told her that I wasn't interested in being right anymore, I just wanted our marriage to work. We made a decision to stay together and from that day until this, we have humbled ourselves before God to ensure that the very pride that caused us to rebel against the marriage covenant would never be able to rear its ugly head in our marriage again.

Humility is the opposite of pride. Thus, we used the master key of humility to ensure that we did not seek our own way in our relationship. I sought to put her first, and she sought to put me first. That took a lot of humility on both of our parts. Anyone can seek his/her own way, but it takes a very mature person (which you are) to shelve his/her own desires and make the desires of his/her spouse the priority. It doesn't always feel good to have to play second fiddle, especially when you feel you are right. However, I didn't care **who** was right; I only cared about **what** was right and being together in our relationship until death do us part was right. If you are seeking to have your own way, you are a catalyst to disastrous outcomes in your marriage.

Adopt this philosophy for your spiritual life and everything—not just your marriage—will work better: "It's not about me." Simple. "It's not about me." Everything in your Christ-centered life should be about giving glory to God and demonstrating the love of Christ and about submitting your will to Christ. This is true in how you do your job, manage your life, raise your kids, serve your neighbors, minister to your community and love your spouse. "It's not about me." It's all about Christ. You are the living expression of God's love which means His priorities should be yours in everything you do. Period.

Today, do everything you can to make sure you are putting the needs of your spouse before your own needs. Let me warn you, however, that this is easier said than done, especially when everything in you will make you feel like your spouse is getting what they want and you aren't getting anything in return. Nevertheless, you must trust the Word of God and the principles that I am sharing with you in order for this to work. The principles work. You must reap when you sow.

Often, when we are flying on the ministry's jet and there is inclement weather, I take the opportunity to go into the cockpit. I have learned that when you can't see a foot ahead of you, you must rely on the instruments before you and the voice of the control tower in your ear. Sometimes it feels like you are disoriented or lost, but if the instrumentation says you are on course, then you are. You must totally rely on the instrumentation that is onboard to navigate you to a safe landing, regardless of what appears to be happening. This equipment is there for a reason and it has been installed to ensure a safe landing. Similarly, God has equipped all of us with what it takes to navigate our way to a safe landing in marriage. Humility is a major part of the equipment that is installed in each of us in order to ensure a blessed relationship. He has already given us everything that pertains to life and Godliness. Use it!

One of the most misinterpreted and misunderstood passages of Scripture has to be Ephesians 5:22 which reads, "Wives, submit yourselves unto your own husbands, as unto the Lord" (KJV). For centuries, these words have been used to dominate and abuse the beautiful order of marriage that God ordained. Does this sound familiar? "I'm the man and you're supposed to do what I say. The Bible says that you're supposed to submit to your husband." However, truth be told, and the truth should be told, submission is a two-way street. Submission has more to do with responsibility and accountability than it does with power or authority. After all, I run everything in my home. I run the vacuum cleaner, I run the dishwasher ... simply everything!

Think about it. The Father, the Son, and the Holy Spirit are one. They are equal, but distinctly and uniquely different. We see in Scripture that Jesus willingly submitted His will to His Father's will. Submission is not about *equality*; it's about *equity* which is based on the rules and order of marriage as designed by God. It's impossible to have unity (oneness) where there is no submission.

In Ephesians 5:22-24, God says that wives are to submit themselves to their own husbands "as unto the Lord," and they are to be subject to their husbands "in everything." If this one truth is accepted and practiced in a marriage and an equally important truth is misunderstood, ignored, or rebelled against, that marriage falls short of God's Will. By commanding that the wife submit to her husband, God has placed on husbands the responsibility for all decisions.

If a man is wise, he will take his wife as a full partner and help her develop her talents. If he really loves her, as opposed to considering her as a possession to serve his every desire, he will dedicate himself to helping her develop as a Godly woman.

Wives submit? If a husband is loving her as God intends him to love her, he will be so unselfishly and humbly dedicated to her good and so considerate of God's Will for her as well as her wishes, desires and opinions, that she will hardly realize that she is in submission. This is the beauty of biblical roles in marriage. If biblical truth is held in balance and practiced, the husband will be dedicated to doing good for her and she will gratefully let him lead.

Scriptures (MSG)

Ephesians 5:21-24 "Out of respect for Christ, be courteously reverent to one another. Wives, understand and support your husbands in ways that show your support for Christ. The husband provides leadership to his wife the way Christ does to his church, not by domineering but by cherishing. So just as the church submits to Christ as he exercises such leadership, wives should likewise submit to their husbands. "

1 Peter 3:7 "The same goes for you husbands: Be good husbands to your wives. Honor them, delight in them. As women they lack some of your advantages. But in the new life of God's grace, you're equals. Treat your wives, then, as equals so your prayers don't run aground."

Matthew 16:25 "Self-help is no help at all. Self-sacrifice is the way, my way, to finding yourself, your true self."

Scriptures (KJV)

1 Peter 5:5b-6 "Yea, all of you be subject one to another, and be clothed with humility: for God resisted the proud, and giveth grace to the humble. Humble yourselves therefore under the mighty hand of God, that he may exalt you in due time."

James 4:10 "Humble yourselves in the sight of the Lord, and he shall lift you up."

Exercise

Make a list of your top three strengths and the top three strengths of your spouse (e.g. finances, organization, etc.). Based on your lists, discuss with your spouse one of the areas where you will lead and where you will submit with your individual strengths and weaknesses in mind. If this exercise goes quickly for you, continue to expand your list to include additional strengths and weaknesses. Complete this exercise as part of a family meeting with your spouse.

Confession

Husbands: I honor, cherish and love my wife as Christ loves the church. I am a good husband to my wife and I always keep her first.

Wives: I love, respect and support my husband. I am a good wife to my husband, and I always keep him first.

____

____

____

____

____

____

____

____

____

____

____

____

____

DAY 24:

ORDER & HONOR

Order and honor are the foundational twin towers as it relates to marriage. I have never ever seen any organization or institution work without these two principles being firmly in place. Order and honor are absolutely essential in the marriage covenant. God is a God of order. Everything that is not in order is out of order and He is not obligated to be a part of anything that is out of order. To ensure that we have the Spirit of God operating in this union, we must walk in the basics. You've made a decision; you've humbled yourself; now let's get things in order. That is how God's Word directs us, so we know that formula is what will protect us.

The order we are referring to was established in the Word of God concerning marriage. From the very beginning God gave man and woman dominion in the earth to be in charge of everything in the earth. God's order is that you dominate together. He has even established order for the home: 1 Corinthians 11:3 says, "But I would have you know, that the head of every man is Christ; and the head of woman is the man; and the head of Christ is God." This does not mean that the woman is subservient to the man or not allowed to have any say in the home, but this directive simply establishes order and accountability. For too long, this Scripture has been taken out of context in many relationships and the result is that a lot of good marriages have been ruined. Again, the power to define is the power to fulfill. By His Word, God is not obligated to participate in, nor put His seal of approval on, anything that is out of order. There first must be order for Him to participate.

In the Old Testament, Hezekiah almost had his life shortened because there was no order in his house. The minute order was restored, his life was restored. Today I want you to work on respecting one another and bringing your home into Godly order. Think back to the time you first met each other. You would have never dishonored or disrespected your spouse because of the impression you were attempting to establish with him/her. Now that you are married, honor and respect have gone out the window. Most of our grandparents taught us to always extend common courtesy and respect to everyone. At a minimum, we need to exercise this philosophy in our marriages.

Some have thrown off restraint in what they will say and do in the presence of one other. You act out because you no longer honor or respect each other. It's interesting that we will treat our spouse worse than we would our best friend. If I were in your home, you would honor my presence. You would not treat me the way you treat each other and certainly not say what you would say to one another in my presence.

Long before we began pastoring, I can recall when DeeDee and I would be on our way to church totally out of order and disrespecting one another. We would talk about one another and even curse each other out (well, I did all the "cursing"). What's interesting is that the minute we got out of the car and encountered other believers, our demeanors would change. We didn't want to give anyone the impression that we were out of control because we honored what they thought about us more than we honored each other. How did we forget that God was there the entire time? He was in the car with us, just like He is with you in your car and in your home? He's everywhere. If you honor God, you must honor your spouse. We must get back to the place where you will commit to making good impressions and honoring each other. Psalm 26:8 says, "Lord, I have loved the habitation of thy house, and the place where thine honor dwelled." We know that the Holy Spirit operates in atmospheres. Your home must be the place where His Spirit has free reign to abide. Create the atmosphere with music, flowers, and whatever else gets your heart and mind stayed on Christ Jesus. The Holy Spirit operating in your home is key to your family's success.

Remember when you first saw your spouse and thought that this possibly could be the "One?" You stepped up, put on your best smile and put your best foot forward in hopes to lure him/her into a place that he/she would feel the same way about you. You looked good, smelled good, very rarely lost your temper or showed any of the other less than positive traits of your personality. You even said nice things to make him/her fall in love with you. Your designated representative was on full alert! The designated representative is the person that we put out front so that our potential mate *thinks* we are a certain way so that we will be attractive to them and, ultimately, they will agree to partner with us in relationship. How long did that last? At some point, it stopped being important to maintain that impression and reputation, we let our guards down and became casual in our relationship. It is important to note that when you allow yourself to become casual about anything, you open the door to the chance of becoming a casualty of that very same thing.

During one of our MMEZ events, I asked the couples in attendance, "How many of you have never argued with one another?" As you can imagine, very few couples raised their hands. Actually, I believe it was only two of the hundreds of couples that were in attendance. The Holy Spirit told me that the foundational reason we argue with one another is that we have lost the honor and respect that we had for one another in the beginning.

The Holy Spirit put me in remembrance of my relationship with Dr. Frederick K.C. Price. In the many, many years that I have known him, I have never, ever, not even once, argued with him. Rather than dispute anything that he has said or done, I made a decision to maintain order in the relationship and keep him in a position of honor rather than arguing with him. Then, the Holy Spirit drew the parallel between my relationship with Dr. Price and DeeDee. He showed me how I avoided arguing with Dr. Price to maintain a certain position and stature in his eyes, yet I didn't maintain the same impression with DeeDee by avoiding arguing with her. I had stopped honoring her enough to maintain the impression that I gave her of who I was in the first place, even though I fully expected to be with her the rest of my life. Then I realized that if I would give DeeDee the same honor I gave Dr. Price, we never had to argue with one another. At that point, I realized that I had to humble myself to have order and honor in my marriage.

You will not be able to honor your spouse without first humbling yourself. Often seeing our spouse in negative situations and knowing intimate and personal details about him/her can cause us to lose respect for him/her. The Bible says that we all have sinned and come short of the glory of God. A prideful attitude will cause us to act as if we are better than our spouses because we haven't done the things that they have done. We know that this is a trick of the enemy, designed to get our focus off of God and onto our spouse.

Matthew 7:1-5 in the Message Bible says, "Don't pick on people, jump on their failures, criticize their faults— unless, of course, you want the same treatment. That critical spirit has a way of boomeranging. It's easy to see a smudge on your neighbor's face and be oblivious to the ugly sneer on your own. Do you have the nerve to say, 'Let me wash your face for you,' when your own face is distorted by contempt? It's this whole traveling road-show mentality all over again, playing a holier-than-thou part instead of just living your part. Wipe that ugly sneer off your own face and you might be fit to offer a washcloth to your neighbor."

If these attitudes have been prevalent in your marriage, repentance is necessary. Not just an apology or request for forgiveness, although that is important, too. True repentance is about asking for forgiveness and then turning away from the thing for which you are apologizing. We are starting over again. Let's get in faith and demonstrate respect, order and honor, even if it has been abused and/or violated. It's a new day! I know it's work, but it's worth it.

Scriptures (KJV)

Romans 13:7	"Render therefore to all their dues: tribute to whom tribute is due; custom to whom custom; fear to whom fear; honour to whom honour."
Proverbs 15:33	"The fear of the Lord is the instruction of wisdom; and before honour is humility."

Proverbs 21:21 "He that followeth after righteousness and mercy findeth life, righteousness and honour."

Exercises

Go to each other, look each other in the eye and repent for all of the dishonorable actions and words that have been a part of your life. Actually say the words, "I APOLOGIZE for..." Ask specifically for your spouse's forgiveness. (Depending on what your children have seen, you may need to seek their forgiveness as well.)

Get back to honoring each other (i.e., opening doors, saying please, thank you, you're welcome, compliments, etc.); set the first impression again. Initially it will seem almost phony, but practice makes permanent and perfect practice makes perfect. Besides, we walk by faith, not by sight.

Confession

I give honor and respect to my spouse with my words, actions and expressions all the days of my life.

____

____

____

____

____

____

____

____

DAY 25:

GET YOUR PRIORITIES STRAIGHT

It goes without saying that most of us are really, really busy these days. Many of us are overwhelmed by the competing demands of work, bills, family and responsibilities and over and over again I hear people say, "I don't have time for this or that." That's not necessarily true. It's not that you don't *have* time; we all have the exact same total of 24 hours in a day. It's that you haven't *made* time for that activity because it is not a priority in your life and how you handle time is a clear indicator of your priorities. There are many things we can lose and get back, like money. Time, however, is not one of them.

We must learn to respect time, especially since how you handle time is a clear representation of who you are and the level of excellence that you possess and operate under. It creates an impression to others as to your character or lack thereof and reflects your priorities and values. Yesterday we talked about Honor and Order. How you handle time reflects the level of honor that you have for a person. In all the years that I have had appointments and meetings with Dr. Price, I have never been late for any of them. There have been times that I have had to drive rather quickly to arrive on time. Still, I have never been late.

Psalms 90:12 says, "So teach us to number our days, that we may apply our hearts unto wisdom." Teach us to number, 1-2-3, our days. Teach us to prioritize. If your priorities are wrong, then your values are going to be wrong. If someone says that they did not or do not have time for something or someone, they are simply saying that something else is more important to them than the thing or that person. They have prioritized something else as being of greater value than what you want from them. Some have said that they don't have time for prayer. That means they have not prioritized prayer as being valuable enough to their lives to set aside time for it.

The bad news is that time flies. The good news is that you are the pilot. You are in control of this. If the truth is told, and the truth should be told, no matter how booked up and busy we are, we can find time to do exactly what we want to do and what we want to do is always in alignment with our priorities. The challenge comes when our priorities are out of order.

In marriage, there has to be agreement over the priorities of the individuals and the marriage. So often, when I have asked couples to list their priorities for me, they haven't even agreed with each other. How can two walk together unless they are in agreement? Sometimes they are deceived. What I mean is that they have the answer to the priorities question correct and in order, but they're really not operating in alignment with them. There are two things that will give you a correct picture of your priorities: your calendar and your checkbook. Whatever gets your time and your money is what matters most to you.

Who and what gets your time and money? Is God really first in your life, in your home, in your marriage? Does He get your time, attention, and tithes? When God is your first priority, the others tend to easily fall in place.

As we discussed on Day 12, part of your family constitution must deal with the question of priorities. DeeDee and I wrote down everything that was important to us. Then we put them in order by importance. This list of priorities then became part of our Freeman Family Constitution. In our home, we've decided that these are our priorities, in order:

1. God
2. Spouse
3. Children and Immediate Family
4. Service to Church & Others

These are just a guideline, an indication of what we determined our priorities to be. You will need to discuss them and their order for your own family.

When DeeDee and I talk with couples, most often, after God first, their priorities tend to be out of order. This is an area that spouses get turned around most often. They put the children and other family members before their husband and wife and that is simply out of order for what God has ordained. We have already established that what a husband needs from his wife is going to be different than what a wife needs from her husband. Still, after our relationship with God, it is our responsibility to make meeting the needs of our spouse our priority. Then the children and the other areas come after that.

During the conversation about priorities, we always hear couples, especially the wife, talk about the ever-elusive idea of balance. The complaint is that they can't seem to achieve it. They bring up the Scripture in Proverbs 11:1a that says that "a false balance is an abomination unto the Lord." (KJV) They use the Scripture to build a doctrine in their own minds that it's even hopeless to try. This is where your study and meditation on the Word come in. When you read the Scripture in other translations, you get a clearer picture of what God is referring to. For instance, in the Amplified version of the Bible, Proverbs 11:1 says "A false balance and unrighteous dealings are extremely offensive and shamefully sinful to the Lord, but a just weight is His delight." He's not even talking about balancing priorities, yet we use this scripture to beat ourselves up.

Let me help you understand. Any time that God calls for you to do anything, it's going to cause you to have to take some of those same 24 hours, everyone has them, from something else to do it. Why are we trying to balance time between God, our spouse, our kids, our work, etc? That would mean that we would spend 8 hours with work, 8 hours with God, 8 hours with our spouse, and so on and so on. The problem is that we're attempting to achieve static balance when we should really be after a dynamic balance. Static balance simply means that everything gets the exact same amount of time. Dynamic balance means that the time spent on our priorities is based on the ebbs and flows of the other areas of our lives. Remember, there is no condemnation in God. Don't allow the enemy to wreck your plan by making you feel as though you're not good enough because your life is out of balance. We are so serious about this in our ministry that our married partners are only allowed to participate in two areas of ministry. We want to make sure that they are not using their responsibilities to minister as a reason to ignore other priorities and responsibilities.

Here are some things to think about: (1) Is your spouse before your boss or your co-workers when it comes to who gets your attention first? (2) Before you start volunteering in the community, have you checked to make sure your own household is running the way it's supposed to and (3) do your children have all the time and concern they need from you? Priorities are one of the most important keys to a successful life.

Scripture(MSG)

Matthew 6:30-33	"If God gives such attention to the appearance of wildflowers—most of which are never even seen—don't you think he'll attend to you, take pride in you, do his best for you? What I'm trying to do here is to get you to relax, to not be so preoccupied with *getting,* so you can respond to God's *giving.* People who don't know God and the way he works fuss over these things, but you know both God and how he works. Steep your life in God-reality, God-initiative, God-provisions. Don't worry about missing out. You'll find all your everyday human concerns will be met."
Matthew 10:34-39	"Don't think I've come to make life cozy. I've come to cut – make a sharp knife-cut between son and father, daughter and mother, bride and mother-in-law – cut through these cozy domestic arrangements and free you for God. Well-meaning family members can be your worst enemies. If you prefer father or mother over me, you don't deserve me. If you prefer son or daughter over me, you don't deserve me. If you don't go all the way with me, through thick and thin, you don't deserve me. If your first concern is to look after yourself, you'll never find yourself. But if you forget about yourself and look to me, you'll find both yourself and me."

Scripture(KJV)

III John 2 — "Beloved, I wish above all things that thou mayest prosper and be in health, even as thy soul prospereth."

Exercise

What are the top priorities for your family? Look at your calendar and checkbook to see if there is alignment. If not, discuss with your spouse ways to get your priorities straight.

For one week, monitor the ways in which you allow other things to take higher priority over your marriage and family. For example, keep track of how many times **YOU** are late for family engagements, athletic games and practices or school play rehearsals. Keep track of key activities **YOU** miss, such as kissing your spouse goodnight or tucking your children into bed. Learn from your mistakes and vow to make your spouse and family a priority.

Confession

My priorities are in order and my household functions the way God ordained as I seek first the kingdom of God and His righteousness, all these things will be added unto me.

____

____

____

____

____

____

DAY 26:

PRAY AND FAST

Have you ever heard the saying, "The family that prays together stays together?" We hear it a lot because it's true, to some degree. Obviously it takes more than prayer alone, yet prayer has the ability to strengthen a marriage and unite a family, mainly because prayer requires a certain posture of humility. You cannot go to God with a spirit of anger, resentment, bitterness or pride. Prayer requires that we put aside our "issues" and humbly present ourselves to the Father. Demonstrating a strong prayer life for children also enhances their stability and increases their faith. Children need to hear and see that God answers prayer.

Husbands, as spiritual leaders in your home, it is your Godly obligation to pray with and for your family. Inherent in leadership is the idea that others are following, and leaders should be taking them where they need to go. Let me say this differently. As the God-ordained leader in your household, turn around and look behind you. If your wife is not there, if your children are not there, you are not leading, you are simply taking a walk. You must set an example worthy of following and there is no better place for a husband and father to lead his wife and children than to the throne room of God through prayer. Early in our marriage, especially when our children were growing up in our home, we prayed together daily. Now, as our schedules have changed so drastically, we have separate times of prayer, yet the foundation of prayer is in place throughout our family. We also have a prayer board where we post all of the things that we are in faith for so that we can individually take time to pray over those needs and desires.

It is vital to understand the importance and the purpose of prayer. We pray to connect and communicate with God – not just offer up a wish list of the things we want or desire. We pray to God the Father by the power of the Holy Spirit, in the name, power and authority of Jesus. Prayer is a dialogue – not a monologue. Yes, we should praise, worship and offer our petitions or requests to God; then we should wait to hear His response. Think about the last time you prayed. Did you just talk or did you also take the time to listen and hear what God had to say? This is where we receive our marching orders, our clear instructions. Most of us rush through prayer and devotion so quickly we actually miss out on the benefits of spending time with God. We are so busy being busy that we forget to be still. We forget that God's voice is the still, quiet voice that speaks to our hearts.

DeeDee and I are big supporters of Christian counseling. However, outside of prayer, everything else you do will be ineffective. Prayer is a bridge that leads to the presence of God. In the presence of God we find healing, forgiveness, deliverance and peace. Prayer is the best wedding gift that God could have given us to navigate the sometimes challenging circumstances of marriage.

Men, there is no arguing that women like diamonds, flowers and expensive gifts; but there is a lot to be said for the gift of prayer. The way to truly minister to a woman's heart is to allow her to see you interceding in prayer for your marriage, for her specifically, and for your family. Let her see you send up a prayer to heaven and get an answer back on earth. This reinforces her confidence in your ability to provide and care for her – because you have access and influence with the Almighty God. Let's see a dozen roses beat that! Besides, often we are limited in our ability to truly understand our wives outside of heavenly intervention and translation. We will strive an entire lifetime to get to know our wives. Fortunately, if you keep your heavenly ears open, you can download divine interpretations of exactly what to say and how to say it so that your love for your wife will be evident.

Women, quite frankly, the basic needs of men are pretty straightforward. Men want and need to be fed: physically, sexually and psychologically (ego and all). The first two needs are fairly straightforward, so let's talk about how to feed your husband's psychological needs. Men desire respect and admiration from their wives. If you are constantly criticizing and talking down to your husband instead of uplifting him, he will seek out other ways to fulfill that need. Knowing that you—his wife—are praying for him and encouraging him is the emotional boost he needs to become the man God created him to be. Become his personal corner man, his very own cheerleader. (For added leverage, you can even dress up like a cheerleader, complete with pompoms.) You are the perfect helper (Genesis 2:18) created for God's purpose in his life. If you neglect to pray for your husband, you will find him lacking in the area of psychological fulfillment and lacking in the ability to be the best husband he can be for you.

When you pray, make sure that you don't violate your prayers with your actions or conversation. Ensure that you pray in faith, using the four functioning components of faith–Believing, Receiving, Speaking, and Acting—discussed on Day 17.

Christians should pray and fast – consistently. There are a lot of misconceptions about fasting, so here's what it is. And here's what it is not.

Fasting is not a crash diet. Fasting is not something you do to demonstrate your level of spirituality to others. Fasting is not routine. Fasting is not to be taken lightly.

Fasting is focused and intentional restraint from physical appetites (usually from food) in the pursuit of establishing a clear communication channel with God and strengthening your relationship with Christ. Fasting removes the focus from our physical needs such as eating, drinking, sexual satisfaction, media and entertainment and redirects it to the spiritual realm where we can access the supernatural and connect with God.

There are dozens of examples of fasts detailed in the Bible throughout the Old and New Testament. In many instances, fasting was used as a rallying cry to unite forces leading into battle. Fasting was used to sanctify a family, army or tribe to be used by God. Fasting was used to unite members in the family of God toward a common goal or purpose. It inflicts discipline upon the flesh and reins our appetites into submission and fasting also makes us mindful of the abundance we have – and reminds us to be grateful.

Our son Joshua was late coming home one evening. Just as I started asking questions about where he was, the phone rang. The officer told us that our son, DeeDee's only boy, had been arrested and was being charged with attempted murder. This was a huge blow to our family. We immediately began to pray, both together and apart. I fasted and we called those charges "cancelled." Ultimately, after walking through the situation in faith, all of the charges were dropped and our son was released from jail. There is infinite power in the prayer of agreement.

The combination of fasting and prayer is powerful. Prayer, fasting and agreement in marriage are phenomenal.

In general, there are three main categories of fasting: absolute, regular and partial. An absolute fast is continual abstinence from all food and drink for a set period of time. A regular fast consists of abstaining from food, but drinking plenty of water to prevent dehydration. A partial fast encompasses abstaining from food or drink or other activities that might distract your attention from spiritual matters for a specified range of time, e.g., no TV from 8 p.m. to 8 a.m. while also sacrificing meals for a day to focus on prayer and spending time with God.

Regardless of the type of fast you undertake, the priority should be on spending time in the presence of God. Fasting is used to clarify purpose and priorities in your life and it's also a powerful weapon in your arsenal for spiritual warfare.

Scriptures (MSG)

Matthew 6:16-18 "When you practice some appetite-denying discipline to better concentrate on God, don't make a production out of it. It might turn you into a small-time celebrity but it won't make you a saint. If you 'go into training' inwardly, act normal outwardly. Shampoo and comb your hair, brush your teeth, wash your face. God doesn't require attention-getting devices. He won't overlook what you are doing; he'll reward you well."

Mark 11:23-25 "Jesus was matter-of-fact: 'Embrace this God-life. Really embrace it, and nothing will be too much for you. This mountain, for instance: Just say, 'Go jump in the lake' – no shuffling or shilly-shallying—it's as good as done. That's why I urge you to pray for absolutely everything, ranging from small to large. Include everything as you embrace this God-life, and you'll get God's everything. And when you assume the posture of prayer, remember that it's not all asking. If you have anything against someone, forgive – only then will your heavenly Father be inclined to also wipe your slate clean of sins.'"

Scriptures (KJV)

Deut. 4:29-31 "But if from thence thou shalt seek the LORD thy God, thou shalt find him, if thou seek him with all thy heart and with all thy soul. When thou art in tribulation, and all these things are come upon thee, even in the latter days, if thou turn to the LORD thy God, and shalt be obedient unto his voice; (For the LORD thy God is a merciful God;) he will not forsake thee, neither destroy thee, nor forget the covenant of thy fathers which he sware unto them."

Psalms 25:4 "Shew me thy ways, O LORD; teach me thy paths."

Matthew 6:33 "But **seek ye first** the kingdom of God, and his righteousness; and all these things shall be added unto you."

1 Thess. 5:17 "Pray without ceasing."

Exercises

Commit to beginning each day in prayer; bless your spouse; declare what you want to see in their lives. (If you have children, make sure they are included, when possible. Children do what you do, not what you say.) Watch and see how much closer your family becomes when it unites together in prayer.

Discuss and agree on a period of time to jointly fast and pray with your spouse. Record your prayer requests and/or petitions for your marriage and write on the following pages how and when God answers those prayers. Also, write down the instructions or directions He gives to you during your time of prayer and fasting.

Confession

I pray without ceasing for my spouse and he/she experiences the manifestations of those prayers. Fasting and prayer are a regular part of my life.

____

____

____

____

____

____

____

____

DAY 27:

HEALTH - BECOME A MEMBER OF THE 120 CLUB

Your body does not belong to you, so you have no right to abuse, misuse, or neglect it. 1 Corinthians 6:9 states, "What? Know ye not that your body is the temple of the Holy Ghost which is in you, which ye have of God, and ye are not your own?" That means your body belongs to God. Furthermore, we learn in 1 Corinthians 7:4 that the husband's body belongs to the wife and the wife's body belongs to the husband, so it is your responsibility to make sure you nourish and protect your body on behalf of your spouse's needs and their reliance on you to live a long, healthy and fruitful life with him/her.

Getting married is not just about saying, "I do." It's about being an active, engaged participant in each other's lives. As we discussed on Day 25, there's more to life than just work and church - church and work – and then sleeping in late on the weekends. Make moving your body a priority. Get out and have some fun. Grab your wife by the hand and take her for a walk to both get some exercise and spend some time together. As a matter of fact, DeeDee and I committed to each other that we would stay under a certain weight for our entire marriage. We committed to becoming a healthier version of ourselves as a couple. Tone up or slim down to a weight and size that makes you feel comfortable, confident and, dare I say, sexy! Do the work with your spouse to show that as a couple, you are healthier and more attractive to one another. As an added benefit, studies have shown that when you exercise, your body releases certain hormones and pheromones that increase your attraction to your mate and your personal desire for sex. So, in the process of getting there, you will reignite the fire in your marriage – like at the beginning of the relationship when your husband couldn't keep his hands off you or your wife couldn't keep her eyes off you. An investment in your health will definitely yield a positive return in your marriage.

God designed man to live 120 years. This is proven in Genesis 6:3, "Then God said, "I'm not going to breathe life into men and women endlessly. Eventually they're going to die; from now on they can expect a life span of 120 years." (MSG) (This fact has even been confirmed scientifically. Many dentists have gone on record saying that our teeth were designed to last 120 years.) We should set our goals in alignment with the word of God so we should have a goal of living 120 years. Not just to be able to say that we lived that long, although that is a great accomplishment. God has a very specific, 120-year plan and purpose for our lives. A large part of that purpose is to serve Him by helping bring salvation to the world. Can you imagine how much more we as Christians could accomplish for kingdom's sake if we not only lived all those years, but also served him faithfully all of those?

Unfortunately, Christians are more famous for being overweight and unhealthy and end up, on average, dying between the ages of 60 to 80, which is an absolute injustice and misrepresentation of God and His promises to His children. We dig our graves with our teeth, often at church! Churches traditionally are the place with the most fish fries, cook-outs, fried dinner plates. The highest levels of diabetes and obesity can be found within the walls of God's house. What kind of witnesses are we to God's promise of health and healing if we can barely walk up a flight of stairs without passing out? The world is looking to the church for leaders and we are failing miserably. God has called us to be good soldiers and that means ready, willing and able to withstand and sustain a fight. It's not good enough just to have a spiritual defense. We also need to be in good enough health to go out on the spiritual battle fields or the ministry mission fields and get the job done on behalf of our heavenly Father.

If you and your spouse have poor eating or lifestyle habits, now is as good a time as any to change your ways, not just because you want to lose weight or fit in to a certain outfit. Change your habits because you want to live your life and portray a Godly example for your spouse and children. We must take control of our health so that our bodies will be able to sustain our spirits long enough for us to do what God created us to do. Remember, we gave our all, including our bodies, to God. It's time now to make sure that our bodies are a true representation of His goodness and, just like the things we do to glorify God, we want to make sure that our bodies glorify God as well.

Scripture

1 Corinthians 6:19b "Or didn't you realize that your body is a sacred place, the place of the Holy Spirit? Don't you see that you can't live however you please, squandering what God paid such a high price for? The physical part of you is not some piece of property belonging to the spiritual part of you. God owns the whole works. So let people see God in and through your body."

Exercise

Share with your spouse your health goals and work together to create a plan to help you to achieve them individually and as a couple. Discuss the adjustments necessary to support your goals. How will you begin to cook? What exercises will you do? Will you work out together or individually? Write down the top three changes that you will make to begin moving your health in the direction of longevity.

Also, look for ways to add exercise to your current routine. For instance, walking up the stairs instead of taking the elevator; walking to school to meet the kids rather than driving, etc.

Confession

Lord, you said with long life will You satisfy me, and I receive Your promise, God, to live 120 years in health and prosperity.

____

____

____

____

____

____

____

____

____

____

DAY 28:

SEASONS - THE ONLY CONSTANT IS CHANGE

Seasons are periods of time in time. The more seasons you can get control of, the more control you will have of your life and your marriage. The Word of God says in Ecclesiastes 3:1 that "To everything there is a season, and a time to every purpose under the heaven." Each of our lives experiences the equivalent of spring, summer, fall, and winter – in various forms of trials, challenges, occasions, successes and accomplishments. People and circumstances come and go in our lives; invariably, seasons change.

Even the seasons of your marriage will change, yet inside of every season is an opportunity. Opportunities must be seen and seized. You may even have to swim out to the ship to seize an opportunity, rather than waiting for the ship to come in. Yes, things may start out romantic and passionate... driven by excitement and the newness of the relationship...but ultimately, those feelings and emotions will morph into routine and familiarity. It is the responsibility of both individuals in a marriage to maintain the relationship and work to make sure they don't take each other for granted or allow the marriage to falter.

There may be a season when it's just the two of you and the major responsibilities in the relationship are just to each other. Then there may be a season of child bearing and child rearing where responsibilities are split and it becomes harder to focus on the needs of your spouse, because the needs of your children are so great. Then the children leave and it becomes time to reintroduce yourself to your spouse. I remember even stretching my hand out to DeeDee and saying, "Hi, I'm Mike." Even after the children are older, many couples find themselves caring for aging parents whose needs may include physical, emotional, medical and financial assistance or support. It is through these seasons that many couples drift apart and wake up one day to realize that they hardly know each other.

I often say, "You must sow where you want to grow and go." If you want to excel professionally, then you must "sow" or spend time learning and improving your skill set in order to excel in your vocation. If you want to improve your golf game, then hitting the course once or twice a year won't cut it. You have to work with a professional, practice your swing, establish a routine schedule and commit to getting better. If you want to improve your marriage, you cannot sit on the sidelines and wait for your spouse to change. It doesn't work that way. You must sow where you want to grow. That means you have to listen more, communicate better, and go above and beyond the call of duty to meet your spouse's needs and exceed his/her expectations. You have to plant something if you want to reap a harvest. Sowing and reaping is one of God's established principles in His Word. All you have to do is work the Word, because the Word works.

Finally, seasons are determined by revelation and truth, not by clocks. Don't be distracted, dismayed or discouraged by the world's timing and seasons. Allow your steps to be ordered by the Lord, and He will direct and uphold you in His timing. If you are reading this book, then it's your time and it's your season for a great *Marriage Made EZ.*

If you don't like the season that you and your marriage are in, then change it. God has the best intentions for your life. It's up to you to find out what it takes to reap the blessings of His promises.

Even though, while we're in the midst of them, challenges seem to last forever, the truth is that "trouble don't last always," and that behind every cloud there really is a silver lining. Because we're in Christ, we have the blessed assurance that "all things work together for good for them who love God and are called according to His purpose." (Romans 8:28).

Like it or not, life is filled with challenges, trials, and tribulations. Our goal is to weather each storm as it comes, learn the intrinsic lesson of that storm, then grow, mature and apply that wisdom elsewhere. After all, it's not the storm that takes us out, it's our own inconsistency of not following through in spite of the storm. Truly, it's not the storm; it's the breach in your faith, just like when Hurricane Katrina devastated New Orleans. It wasn't the storm as much as it was the breach in the levee that caused all of the destruction.

In the midst of a real physical or emotional storm, many of us flail about and get tossed to and fro like a ragdoll. However, we're supposed to be steadfast, unmovable and always abounding in the work of the Lord. Steadfastness – an unbreakable, spiritual lifeline. Study 1 Corinthians 15:58. Tell yourself that you have what it takes to go the distance and overcome trials and tribulations. Study and meditate on Hebrews 6:19.

Often, challenges present the perfect opportunity for husbands and wives to come together as a united front. Too many times, when hard times arrive, the problem drives a rift between the spouses and they end up attacking each other instead of attacking the problem. That's a trick of the enemy. Don't let the devil deceive you into turning against each other. Remember, greater is He that's in you than he that's in the world. DeeDee and I have a *Marriage Made EZ* because of our unrelenting tenacity. Webster's defines tenacity as the quality of holding fast; characterized by keeping a firm hold; highly retentive; pertinacious, persistent, stubborn or obstinate. Tenacity will give you the strength to look opposition in the face and know, beyond the shadow of a doubt, that you cannot fail.

When challenges arise, focus your attention on responding to them based on the Word of God. You have power and authority in Jesus' name to speak life or death into a situation. If you have influence in the situation and don't use it, then you are positioned to be influenced. Make sure you exert your Godly influence in all situations.

Scriptures (KJV)

Psalm 18:2	"The LORD is my rock, and my fortress, and my deliverer; my God, my strength, in whom I will trust; my buckler, and the horn of my salvation, and my high tower."
Psalm 23:1	"The Lord is my shepherd; I shall not want."
Hebrews 6:19	"Which hope we have as an anchor of the soul, both sure and stedfast, and which entereth into that within the veil;"

Jeremiah 29:11 "For I know the thoughts that I think toward you, saith the Lord, thoughts of peace and not of evil, to give you an expected end."

Galatians 6:9 "And let us not be weary in well doing: for in due season we shall reap, if we faint not."

Exercise

Describe some things that you did a year or so ago and how they have affected who you are today. How has your relationship with the Lord changed? How has your relationship with your spouse been affected? Now describe the person you plan to be next year. Discuss your plan for growing into that person with your spouse.

Think about a difficult situation that you overcame in your marriage and take time out to praise God for the victory! Just like David used his past victories to overcome his present situations, you can do the same.

Confession

I praise God because I am fearfully and wonderfully made in His image, and I have what it takes to go the full journey through my trials and tribulations. I will not give up during the difficult seasons in my marriage, rather I will trust God and stand on His promises. I refuse to be weary in doing well cause I know that in due season I will reap, if I faint not, because God has a plan for me and my spouse.

____

____

____

DAY 29:

LOVE - LOVE IS WHAT LOVE DOES

To be accurate, "love" is not simply an emotion; it is ability. Love is an action word: the ability to accept, give, serve, honor and embrace – in spite of other factors or circumstances. Love is the ability to overlook wrongdoings and shortcomings and relinquish the need or desire to be right. Love empowers your ability to put someone else's needs ahead of your own. Love considers the big picture and the long-term consequences, not just the temporary moment or the short-term situation. Love is what makes you hang in there when everything else says let go. (1 Corinthians 13:4-8)

The New Testament of the Bible was originally written in Greek. In the Greek language, the single word "*love*" does not fully express its intended meaning, thus there are four words used to express love: *agape, phileo, eros and storge.*

- *Agape* is the highest form of love that we as Christians should have for everyone; unconditional love for no other reason than it's the right thing to do.

- *Phileo* is brotherly love – the love that we share with our friends.

- *Eros* is the erotic type of love that is based on strong attraction that often results in sexual intimacy (designed only to be evident in a marriage relationship).

- *Storge* is the familial love (blood is thicker than water).

Although each type of love has its specific application, all four must be present in your relationship with your spouse in order to have a *Marriage Made EZ.* If you find that any of them are missing in your marriage, then you must exercise your faith and stand on the Word of God that says that if any of you lack wisdom, let him ask of God, that giveth to all men liberally . . . and it shall be given him (James 1:5). He will show you ways to bring back the fire of love to your marriage.

One of the biggest misconceptions about love is that it should always feel good. Without question, although love can produce a wonderful feeling, love isn't always convenient. Love is not just puppies and rainbows, tingling sensations and passion. Sometimes, love means making tough choices and not getting your own way. However, love is always in search of fulfilling the greater good, the needs of others. One of the biggest misunderstandings in marriage is how does one spouse show love to the other. Often we want to communicate our love to them in the way that we want to be loved, which often is not in a way that they can receive. You must love your spouse the way they want to be loved.

If you want to know how you're doing in the love department, ask God first. God is love and He will freely tell you. Just be open to receive from Him. Then, ask your spouse, the recipient of your love, if you dare. Be careful though. You may not like the answers that you get. Most of us fall way short of truly meeting the needs of others around us – especially those who depend on us. We spend a lot of time giving our best to our bosses, clients, congregants and friends and then give what's left over to our spouse and kids. That's not right. That's not fair. That's not scriptural. Often we say we love, but the purported recipient of that love can't receive it. The Bible says that where your treasure is there will be your heart also. If I were to take your checkbook or debit card statement, I could follow the trail from your bank account to the things that are most important to you. Would the trail lead to your spouse? To your hobby? To your church?

In right order, we should absolutely give our best to God, our spouse and then our children. We give first to God because He is our sole source provider and is worthy of our obeisance. We give to our spouse because we made a holy covenant with them in the presence of God to love, honor and cherish them in good times and bad. We give next to our children because they are the offspring and the product of our union in Christ. (This is going to help somebody.) If you are not taking care of home first, you may need to realign your priorities or resign from any competing responsibilities, even the deacon board, hospitality committee, praise team or ministry leadership, until you get your priorities right before God. You have no spiritual right to neglect your family in favor of elevating your personal ministry duties. Effective ministry begins at home.

It can be a very rewarding experience to love through giving. As a matter of fact, the Bible shares a precedent for love through giving: "For God so loved the world, that he GAVE his only begotten Son, that whosoever believeth on him should not perish, but have everlasting life" - John 3:16. By His example, love is a verb – an action word. Some have said, "I'd take a bullet for my spouse" and we would. What I don't understand is that if

you would take a bullet, then why won't you take out the trash? Why won't you take your wife on a vacation? Why won't you rub his shoulders or have dinner ready when he comes home from a long day at work?

In the 90s, a group sang a song with a verse that says, "If you love me, like you say you do, won't you show me, just how much you do." Often your marriage challenges would be minimized, if not totally eliminated, by something as simple as assuring your spouse, with your actions, that you recognize their worth and value and reminding them that your love for them is not simply a product of passion, but a product of the purpose of God in their life. Find out what your spouse's needs are and minister to them ... every day and in every way. Find a way to make sure they know that they're important to you. Where there seems to be no way, make a way. It is your ministry responsibility to your spouse.

<u>Scriptures (KJV)</u>

Ephesians 5:25	"Husbands, love your wives, even as Christ also loved the church, and gave himself for it;"
John 15:13	"Greater love hath no man than this, that a man lay down his life for his friends."
1 Corinthians 13:4-8	"[4]Charity suffereth long, and is kind; charity envieth not; charity vaunteth not itself, is not puffed up, [5]Doth not behave itself unseemly, seeketh not her own, is not easily provoked, thinketh no evil; [6]Rejoiceth not in iniquity, but rejoiceth in the truth; [7]Beareth all things, believeth all things, hopeth all things, endureth all

things. [8]Charity never faileth: but whether there be prophecies, they shall fail; whether there be tongues, they shall cease; whether there be knowledge, it shall vanish away."

Scriptures (AMP)

1 Peter 3:1-7: "[1]Likewise, ye wives, be in subjection to your own husbands; that, if any obey not the word, they also may without the word be won by the conversation of the wives; [2]While they behold your chaste conversation coupled with fear. [3]Whose adorning let it not be that outward adorning of plaiting the hair, and of wearing of gold, or of putting on of apparel; [4]But let it be the hidden man of the heart, in that which is not corruptible, even the ornament of a meek and quiet spirit, which is in the sight of God of great price. [5]For after this manner in the old time the holy women also, who trusted in God, adorned themselves, being in subjection unto their own husbands: [6]Even as Sara obeyed Abraham, calling him lord: whose daughters ye are, as long as ye do well, and are not afraid with any amazement. [7]Likewise, ye husbands, dwell with them according to knowledge, giving honour unto the wife, as unto the weaker vessel, and as being heirs together of the grace of life; that your prayers be not hindered."

1 Peter 4:8	"Above all things have intense and unfailing love for one another, for love covers a multitude of sins [forgives and disregards the offenses of others]."

Scriptures (MSG)

Proverbs 4:7	"Wisdom is the principal thing; therefore get wisdom: and with all thy getting get understanding."
Proverbs 15:1	"A gentle response defuses anger, but a sharp tongue kindles a temper-fire."
1 Corinthians 7:2-5	"It's good for a man to have a wife, and for a woman to have a husband. Sexual drives are strong, but marriage is strong enough to contain them and provide for a balanced and fulfilling sexual life in a world of sexual disorder. The marriage bed must be a place of mutuality—the husband seeking to satisfy his wife, the wife seeking to satisfy her husband. Marriage is not a place to 'stand up for your rights.' Marriage is a decision to serve the other, whether in bed or out. Abstaining from sex is permissible for a period of time if you both agree to it, and if it's for the purposes of prayer and fasting—but only for such times. Then come back together again. Satan has an ingenious way of tempting us when we least expect it."

Exercises

Ask yourself the question, what can I do to most clearly communicate my love to my spouse? How can I best serve God and make this a better marriage? Ask your spouse the same questions. Write your answers on the following pages, and then follow up with the corresponding action.

Confession

Father, I thank you that the love of God has been shed abroad in my heart and I love just like You do, unselfishly and unconditionally, with no strings attached. I communicate love to my spouse in a way that they understand.

Read 1 Corinthians 13 and make it personal by using "I".

___

___

___

___

___

___

___

___

___

___

___

___

DAY 30:

LOVE - GIVE MORE THAN YOU GET

Your giving determines your love towards a certain thing. Matthew 6:21 says, "For where your treasure is, there will your heart be also." Give a little, you love a little. Give a lot, you love a lot. Giving determines your obedience, your vested interest and is the greatest demonstration of love in your life. The amount of time and resources you give is reflected in your calendar and your checkbook and can be used to determine your commitment to anything. Whether you're giving money or of yourself, the principles are the same. And, your giving will get you more out of your marriage than you are currently getting.

Did you balk at the idea when you saw the subtitle above, "Give More Than You Get?" If so, it's understandable. Our human nature is hardwired for self-preservation and to get all we can – sometimes at any cost. You've got to know, we can cover a multitude of imperfections in our lives by giving, just as 1 Peter 4:8 says, "And above all things have fervent charity among yourselves: for charity shall cover the multitude of sins." That's the secret.

Do you ever get tired of giving? Before you answer that question, I need to draw your attention to the fact that there is a definitive difference between giving and spending. Spending is about you;

it's selfish. Giving is about others; it's selfless. The devil has no problem with our spending. When we give, God puts His "super" on our "natural" to create supernatural harvests. The prodigal son spent all of his money and no one would give to him because he hadn't given to anyone else. Giving gets you the God-quality of life. It is a heart issue, because your hand is an extension of your heart. Giving is God's plan for increase.

Now, back to the question: do you ever get tired of giving? I know sometimes it seems like everybody wants or needs something. You give all you have at work and at home. Then you go to church and somebody is asking you to give even more. Then, the kids need you to give them money for the mall and their school or PTA wants you to give for the annual fundraiser. Then there's a disaster somewhere in the country and people victimized by a situation and need others to give and offer support. Then there are the commercials and infomercials on television that show some desperate situation where you once again need to what? You guessed it... give.

Admittedly, there is a lot going on in the world and there are a lot of reasons to give. But the most important reason to give to any cause is in obedience to God's Word. *Give* and it shall be given unto you. For God so loved the world that He *gave*. It is more blessed to *give* than to receive. And so on, and so forth. Strangely enough, more important than your method of giving, God is concerned with your MOTIVE for giving. You must be flowing in your agape love (as discussed on Day 29) when you give. Not giving for getting. We also know that you cannot reap where you have not sown. God placed everything we need inside a seed. He went as far as to say we shall know a tree by its fruit. If the fruit is no good, the root is no good either.

If you want to get something out of *Marriage Made EZ,* then you must be willing to give something. You must be willing to give more time, energy, resources, attention, fasting and prayer to make your marriage work.

When DeeDee and I made a commitment to stay together "til death do us part," we also made a commitment to give everything it took to repair and restore our marriage until it resembled what we were believing God for.

Giving should come as effortlessly as breathing. Although it might take some practice to get used to the idea, there are blessings tied to giving that might hold the answer you've been waiting for. When you commit to give up self and humble yourself before God, then He has an unobstructed pathway to channel blessings back into your life.

"At Times, Actions Speak Louder Than Words"

How does your spouse recognize your love in action? This is not a trick question. It focuses on recognizing and understanding the action cues that your spouse gives and receives that relate their love for you. The problem in many marriages arises when spouses show love differently, meaning that they don't recognize the love that their partner is communicating. Your spouse has every right to show you how they receive love and you have every responsibility to show love in a way that they understand.

Basically, love is expressed or interpreted through several areas. According to a popular study, most individuals have one or two primary love languages, although they may exhibit traits or characteristics from all five areas. Some people recognize love when someone shares encouraging words with them, others when their spouse spends time with them; for some, it's the giving of gifts, others, acts of service and still others, physical touch. So if your spouse primarily recognizes that you love them when you spend quality time with them, but you keep touching them, there is a very loud and prominent misunderstanding brewing. You may not understand why your marriage is spiraling into a loveless relationship, but it might be because you are speaking two different languages.

It's important to take time and understand how your spouse feels love and gives love. Remember that quote I shared earlier in the book: "Seek first to understand, then to be understood?" That goes without saying here. If you honestly don't know what your spouse's love language is, then ask! "Honey, what makes you feel special?" Although you might think that providing a nice, big home says, "I love you," what she really needs is to hear the words, "I love you." Although you might think that buying him a new flat screen television shows that you care, he really wants a home-cooked meal. For instance, DeeDee loves cards with personal notes and flowers. Even if I have to note it on my calendar, I make sure that I send her notes and flowers occasionally so that she is reminded of my love for her. It was also important to her that I call in so that she knew where I was and that I was safe. In the beginning, I felt like, I'm a grown man, why am I checking in. Then I realized that doing so was just another way of my communicating my love and respect for my wife.

Pay attention to the obvious signs and signals that your spouse gives off on a daily basis. For some wives, affection and intimacy that don't necessarily lead to sex is a way they recognize and receive love. She wants a hug; she needs a hug; if you want her to feel secure in your marriage, hug her several times every day. A husband's security in the marriage is reinforced when his wife responds positively to his sexual advances. When wives misuse or withhold sex and physical intimacy, it communicates to him that she is no longer interested and doesn't love him. We must be careful because often our actions speak louder than our words.

Men and women are different. God designed us to be different. But just because we're different doesn't mean we cannot relate and communicate. Take time to learn the love language your husband or wife speaks and watch how quickly your marriage will improve.

Scriptures (KJV)

Matthew 6:21	"For where your treasure is, there will your heart be also."
Hebrews 2:1	"Therefore we ought to give the more earnest heed to the things which we have heard, lest at any time we should let them slip."
Luke 6:38	"Give, and it shall be given unto you; good measure, pressed down, and shaken together, and running over, shall men give into your bosom. For with the same measure that ye mete withal it shall be measured to you again."
Acts 20:35	"I have shown you all things, how that so labouring ye ought to support the weak, and to remember the words of the Lord Jesus, how he said, It is more blessed to give than to receive."

Exercise

Find something that your spouse normally does and do it for them. Make sure it is something that they would enjoy having a break from doing.

Confession

I live life beyond myself and look for ways to serve my spouse knowing that God will not forget my labor of love. The purpose of my giving is totally based on my love for God and my spouse.

DAY 31:
COMMITMENT

The first question we ask in our counseling sessions is, "DO YOU WANT YOUR MARRIAGE?!" Most often the answer we get is, "I want my marriage; I just don't want it like this; and if he/she doesn't change, then I don't want it at all." What your spouse needs to know more than anything is that you are committed to making your marriage work and that your marriage working is NOT contingent upon a spouse changing or improving.

I know you are asking, "How is that possible?" It's possible because life is choice-driven and we live or we die by the choices we make. Everything in life is governed by our decisions and choices. Let's look at the definitions of those words:

> **Decide** – [*verb*] to make a final choice or judgment about; to select as a course of action
>
> **Choose** – [*verb*] to select freely and after consideration
>
> www.merriam-webster.com (May 2011)

When it comes to marriage, we have to kill any option that is contrary to our decision to make our marriage work. We must choose to fight for our marriage regardless of what we must endure. That's what DeeDee and I did. God has created all of us as free moral agents. We have free will to reject Jesus or accept Jesus (and all the benefits and promises of living for Him) and our will is the most powerful thing that we possess. So once you decide that your marriage is worth fighting for, come hell, high water, low water or no water at all, you are well on your way to victory. Deuteronomy 30:19 says, "I call heaven and earth to record this day against you, that I have set before you life and death, blessing and cursing: therefore choose life…" Choose life!

Go to the end of the decision – check out the consequence. Is that truly what you want in your future? If so, roll up your sleeves, put on your work clothes and let's do the work and partake in the journey to the marriage that you both desire and deserve.

DeeDee and I decided that we wanted our marriage to work and after that decision was made is when it really seemed like all hell broke loose. However, again, everything worth having is worth fighting for and the fight is won from the very beginning once the decision has been made. We both chose life. Even Jesus Himself decided to redeem us back unto Himself, but that choice was not without a fight. You will inevitably encounter temptation, tests and trials when you make a decision. When you make a decision to lose weight, there will be a fight. When you make a decision to read your Bible, there will be a fight. When you make a decision to love your enemies, there will be a fight. Let's not fool ourselves into believing that things will automatically improve once we make a decision. I am telling you that this is where the fight is won or lost… at the point of your decision. It's a faith fight. So fight the good fight of faith! Remember, we win!

After having made your decision, *you will have to fight. Let me be crystal clear. You must understand* that the only thing that is going to be different about your marriage at this time is your unyielding decision to fight for it. Without any other way out of your marriage, divorce will not be an option. Neither will separation or going back on your promise. We are burning down all bridges. We are eliminating every stick, brick and mortar that would allow you to build a bridge to go back on your decision. From this day forward, the only way to go is forward.

Because He is the living Word of God, God's Word will never contradict His Will. It is the Will of God for your marriage to survive and thrive, in spite of the current divorce rate, in spite of your life's circumstances and in spite of the really bad advice being given about marriage throughout popular culture. Jesus is at the core of your marriage, because He created marriage. Think about what you would do if a very important appliance in your house broke down. You would read the instruction manual, call customer service or the help desk and speak with someone from the manufacturing division. Your marriage is the same way. When you notice that it's not working the way it was designed to work, long before it fails, you should read the Bible, which is the instruction manual (rather than waiting until we have a problem), call on Jesus in prayer, which is the heavenly customer service support center and you should take it to God, the manufacturer, because He knows how to fix it. He knows why He created marriage and how He created it to work. Instead of relying on inadequate advice from people who don't specialize in restoring marriages, just take it straight to the warehouse, because your marriage is under full warranty until "death do you part."

Scripture (KJV)

Galatians 6:9	"And let us not be weary in well doing: for in due season we shall reap, if we faint not."

Philippians 4:13 "I can do all things through Christ which strengtheneth me."

Exercise

Think of challenges that you have overcome in your marriage that seemed difficult at first. Write them on the following pages and praise God for the victory! Apply the same kind of tenacity, the 3 Ps: passion, persistence and perseverance, to your current marital challenges that you have applied to other areas of your life.

Write a short letter to your spouse detailing why it is that you are committed to this marriage. Before bedtime, read it to your spouse, then give it to your spouse.

Confession

Today, I choose life. Today, I choose love. Today, I choose to make my marriage work. Today, I choose to fight. I have decided and, therefore, divorce is not an option. I commit to the principles in this book and to a *Marriage Made EZ* and declare war on divorce. Say it!

____

____

____

____

____

____

____

CLOSING

Congratulations! If you're reading this page, I am assuming that you have gone through this entire book day by day and are firmly on the path to a *Marriage Made EZ.* If that is not the case, go back and start again and read this book as it has been prescribed. If you have, you still can go back through and review the information since repetition is the mother of all learning and faith cometh by hearing and hearing and hearing yet again.

DeeDee and I are proud that you have completed the journey to a *Marriage Made EZ.* We know that your marriage is growing and your relationship is stronger than ever before. Know that this is only the beginning of your journey.

We would also like to take this opportunity to personally extend two invitations to you. First, you're invited to attend any of the *Marriage Made EZ* events that are happening around the world. Visit our website at www.MarriageMadeEZ.com for details. The second invitation is for you to partner with us as we have declared war on divorce. The last page of this book will give you information on the different levels of partnership available to you.

We declare the blessings of God Almighty into your marriage and thank God for your faithfulness to Him and to this ministry.

DR. MICHAEL A. FREEMAN
Spirit of Faith Christian Center
"One Church in Three Locations"
Maryland

Passionate, Edgy, Relatable, Powerful, Funny. These are just some of the words that describe Mike Freeman.

He is a fourth generation pastor and is the founder of Spirit of Faith Christian Center (SOFCC), which is one church with three locations in Maryland. Pastor Freeman has a heart to teach God's people in simplicity and power on how to achieve God's best for their lives. His God-ordained assignment is to minister to the whole man, spirit, soul and body, with special emphasis on faith, family and finances through fellowship.

Founded in 1993, Spirit of Faith Christian Center is one of the fastest growing ministries in our nation. Dr. Michael Freeman is one of the most sought after teachers in the Body of Christ. The demands on his profound understanding of the Word has him traveling throughout the nation, as well as, around the world.

He and his wife Deloris (affectionately known as DeeDee) have also started a ministry that ministers specifically to the covenant of marriage, which is appropriately called *Marriage Made EZ.*

Pastor Freeman also is the President for an internationally known minister's organization, Fellowship of International Word of Faith Ministries (FICWFM), under the leadership of its founder, Apostle Frederick K.C. Price.

Living by Faith is the radio and television broadcast hosted and taught by the Freemans and is aired both nationally and worldwide.

In addition to its three beautiful campuses, Dr. Freeman and Spirit of Faith Christian Center recently purchased 200 acres of land which is the future home of "Faith City," which will contain all the necessary resources to assist him in fulfilling the God-given vision for ministry that God has entrusted to him.

Mike Freeman attributes his success in life and ministry to his standing on Mark 11:24 which says, "What things soever ye desire, when ye pray, believe that ye receive them, and ye shall have them."

His relationship with his wife DeeDee and their three children, Brittney (husband-Kevin), Joshua and Brelyn are an example and blessing to the congregation of SOFCC.

BECOME A PARTNER OF PURPOSE

3 LEVELS OF PARTNERSHIP!!

PLATINUM PLUS: $49 or more MONTHLY
You'll receive the Marriage Made EZ Partner of Purpose monthly resource on DVD, CD and a special gift. Plus, you'll have access to priority event seating and special perks, such as after-event fellowship opportunities for Platinum Plus Partners.

GOLD: $29 MONTHLY
You'll receive the Marriage Made EZ-Newsletter and the Marriage Made EZ DVD and CD Resource each month by mail with additional content exclusive to Marriage Made EZ Partners of Purpose. Plus you'll have access to priority event seating.

SILVER$19: MONTHLY
You'll receive the exclusive monthly E-Newletter from Pastor Mike & Dr. DeeDee Freeman and Marriage Made EZ digital download or CD Resource received by mail and priority seating at all Marriage Made EZ events!!

PARTNER WITH US TODAY!!
WWW.MARRIAGEMADEEZ.COM

CPSIA information can be obtained at www.ICGtesting.com
Printed in the USA
LVOW04s0828250315

431953LV00021B/223/P